FIND YOUR SPRINKLES

CHRIS MOTT

FIND YOUR SPRINKLES

ACKNOWLEDGMENTS

When baking the perfect batch, one needs to surround oneself with a team of amazing people. I consider my collective team to be the best on the planet. I wish to thank my family. The guidance and love that I have received from my dad, mom, Tim, Rodney, and Mindy is truly more than a man could ask for in life. Your constant encouragement and support have propelled me to new heights. To my children, Jordan, Kaley, and Hayden, who have truly rolled with the punches during my reboot process, I love you with all my heart and you are truly the inspiration for this book. To my loving girlfriend, Andrea, you have stood behind me through thick and thin. You have remained steady and never skipped a beat during my quest to find the real me. To my loving friends, you have pushed me to pursue my passion and dreams every step of the way. My cup overflows with friendship, and for that reason alone, I am a blessed man. I love you all.

To Gordon and Lois Hinkley, you were the best second parents and coaches that I could have been blessed with in life. You truly are an inspiration of how to live. Thank you for adding to my sprinkles.

Expertise has been added to the mix to make this dream become a reality. I would like to acknowledge and thank the following individuals for lending their expertise to the project.

Cover Photography	Kyer Wiltshire—Kyer Photography
Cover Design	Jason Wuchenich—PR Pros Incorporated
Audio Direction	Aaron Murphy-Crews
Audio Technician	Lynz Floren
Content Editing	Sue Olszewski
Copy Editing	CreateSpace

FIND YOUR SPRINKLES

TABLE OF CONTENTS

INTRODUCTION

This is your book. It has been written for you. It's been written by someone like you, who understands your challenges. It contains solutions to real-life questions. No matter where you are, this book has found its way into your possession not by chance, but rather for a very specific reason. There's no such thing as coincidence. Everything has been leading you to this point. Often when we look back at the road behind us, the road signs become clear. This book will serve as your clarity. It's your time to stop searching. It's your time to stop yearning for more in life. It's time to start enjoying all that life has to offer. If you've ever wished for the opportunity to start over, to wipe the slate clean, or start with a blank canvas, then let this book be your guide and recipe for success. Once your kitchen is in order, you can then follow the process. You become free to assemble the perfect ingredients. You are free to mix up and bake the perfect batch. Once achieved, you may decorate your life. Sprinkles signify that you have arrived. You grasp and have embraced the recipe for success. Sprinkles allow you to shine. They fuel your quest to find your true destiny in life. Bring on the sprinkles!

I have embarked on a new chapter in life. I am in the midst of a major reboot. Reboot? Yes, I liken it to an old computer, filled with so much garbage that it's just not running at full capacity. We have all witnessed it. The computer gets stuck and freezes up. It finally throws up the white flag and, in its own way, screams, "I surrender! I can do no more." How do you correct this? You turn the switch off, let it sit for a minute, and then you restart. Essentially it's called a "do over." Don't you remember from elementary school? When you didn't like how something came out the first time, you simply called a "do over." Nobody really gave you too much flack for it, as it was an accepted practice. It's okay to start, fail, and start again. After all, we learn through repetition. It's okay to mess up, as mistakes are really the building blocks of the learning process. However, as we grow older, we seem to lose this idea. For some reason, everything has to be perfect every time. Everything has to be perfect the first time, and the "do over" is gone.

As I reboot my life, I am here to tell you from experience, the "do over" is not gone, merely forgotten. You can still call a "do over," reboot, or start over at any point in your life. You just have to have the courage and conviction to do it. Think of life as one giant chalkboard, and you are both the piece of chalk and the eraser. As quickly as you can write something, you can just as easily erase it and start over.

This was my decision. At age forty-one, things were working great in comparison to the woes of others. However, there was something missing. I couldn't quite put my finger on it, as my life was cluttered by so much background noise. You have been there. You know you have. Life is attacking from all directions, almost to the point that you feel paralyzed. Which front do you attack first? In my case, I decided to go drastic, swim upstream, against the conventional current, and eliminate as much background noise as I could.

Before I explain my actions to reboot or to eliminate the background noise, let me first give you the backstory. As I mentioned, I am a forty-one-year-old male. I have lived a wonderful life. My parents were and have been some of the most positive influences in my life. I have three beautiful kids, who I love more than anything. Yes, they are challenging and joyful in the same breath. I'm in a loving relationship with an incredible woman. I own my own home in Silicon Valley, one of the best places to live in the United States. I was married for twelve years and now have been divorced for nine-some-odd years. I now, after much work and time, have a very healthy relationship with my ex-wife. I am successful in my career. I am surrounded by some of the best friends and family that a man could ever hope for, and I am healthy. Given those facts, you may be asking yourself, "How could something be missing?"

Is there something missing in your life? I believe there's something missing in all of us, something is missing in America, and, what is more important, something is missing worldwide. It's about time we found out what it is. The answer will be different for all of us. As we travel life's highway, what's important today will be trivial in the days to come. It's imperative for us to recognize where our priorities are lacking today to repair them in preparation for tomorrow.

If I had to answer the question, it would be that my life was filled with so much that it all became watered down. Take Kool-Aid, for example. You must add just the right amount of water to the mix. If you add too much water, soon you can't taste the mix. On the other hand, if you don't add enough water, then it becomes too strong and you can't stand the taste. It must be the right amount. My life had a bit too much of everything and maybe too little of what was really important. It became watered down. It was lacking the needed punch in some areas and was overwhelmed with flavor in others. If I have learned one thing, it's that when life gets watered down, people start taking certain aspects for granted. So I said, "Enough." Life is too short and too precious not to be appreciated. I decided to reboot.

I created what I like to call a sense of scarcity. It's simple. It's the law of supply and demand. If something is excessively available, it's often viewed as easy to obtain, and in a sense becomes less valuable. If something is harder to find, achieve, or is not as readily available, it becomes sought after and more valuable.

I was always the guy who was everything to everybody. My family has always turned to me in time of crisis. I have been constantly promoted in my career, mainly because I was a calm leader and, in time of trouble, I held steady and got the job done. All admirable qualities; however, when you are everything to everyone, always available, what happens? Yes, as I said, people start taking you for granted. At whose expense? Mine. Life became that pale glass of Kool-Aid that lacked the punch to satisfy.

So I set off on my own course to restore what was missing. It was certainly not the popular thing to do. It created controversy. It went against conventional wisdom, and, what is more important, it was unique. Have you ever heard the expression "Keeping up with the Joneses?" I was leading that life. I was keeping up with every neighbor on the street, and in my neighborhood I was the one with whom others were trying to keep up.

The direction I chose was totally contrary to this lifestyle. I took that theory and threw it out the door. In fact, I literally went out the door with it. I packed my bags from my old life and went in search of the new. What a wild idea. Everyone thought I was nuts. "What are you doing?" "Why are you doing this?" "Have you lost your mind?" Yes, these are the questions that I faced when I decided to move my father, who had lived with me for seven years, to my brother's house. Okay, that wasn't that insane, LOL. These are the questions I faced when I decided to rent my house out to strangers. These are the questions I faced when I sold 90 percent of all my material belongings. These are the questions I faced when I decided to leave the conventional path of America and started calling my home the Silver Bullet. What exactly is a Silver Bullet? It's a 1974 vintage Airstream.

This beautifully engineered trailer was and still is a timeless marvel. Designed by Wally Byam in 1932, the Airstream was a total departure from the normal box trailer. It was a revolutionary and luxurious item way before its time. The Airstream is a classic and is now more popular than ever. How fitting was it, or rather ironic, that I chose to find myself, regain my sprinkles in life, by moving into something so simple? I find it amazingly symbolic. Life in an Airstream proved that not all pleasurable things have to be the biggest; not all pleasurable things have to be new. Some of the best things are the smallest, and some of the best times were when life was a bit simpler; when we all appreciated a simple glass of Kool-Aid just a bit more.

My new home, the Silver Bullet, stood for something that was vanguard. It was a symbol that I was going against the grain. Moving in literally a new direction. Reducing my footprint from three thousand square feet to barely two hundred square feet was a bold move, to say the least. So I took my show on the road. The idea that I could choose my own scenery, have no lawn to mow and no mortgage to pay, was quite appealing. I could simply sit by a stream, beach, redwood grove, or whatever else suited me. I was able to change my scenery with a turn of a key. As a result, I started to flourish while surrounded by some of the most majestic and sturdy trees on the planet, redwood trees. I parked my new life by the most soothing, babbling brook that you could ever imagine. I had made the conscious decision to ease my burden and surround myself by symbols of simplicity, strength, and a never-ending flow of energy. The Airstream, redwoods, and the babbling brook were where I chose to start the reboot!

In the same breath, I was the source of major conversation within my own circle. I became the brunt of many jokes. "Trailer trash" was the new line. You can just imagine that my friends had a field day with this one. Even my girlfriend got into the act. She ordered me a new license plate for the Bullet. It read "HCTPT." This stood for "High Class Trailer Park Trash." I should have prefaced that by explaining that anyone with enough longevity to stay with me must have a very unique sense of humor. My girlfriend certainly fit that bill, and she was ultrasupportive in my quest. This is where commitment and conviction played a huge part. As you can imagine, not all the jokes were delivered with love or as good spirited as hers. It takes a thick skin to stay the course. When everyone is questioning your wisdom or lack thereof, it takes great determination to stand steady in support of your lone conviction. Even that little voice on my shoulder was saying, "What are you doing? Are you a mad man?"

Swimming upstream against the conventional current takes a huge amount of endurance. However, if you have your eyes firmly fixed on the prize, it becomes easier. This was not some spur-of-the-moment decision. I had put much thought into the move. I had attempted to think literally five miles down the road to anticipate all the challenges that would come along with such a drastic change. Throughout it all, I remained focused on what my goal and motivation were: to attain a simpler life, one that had more quality than quantity.

I'm not saying that you need to go sell all of your worldly belongings and leave your conventional life to be happy. For everyone the adjustment will be different. As I take the left fork in the road, you may take the right. There is no right or wrong answer. Only your internal compass can guide you. The only truth is this: no matter what your purpose is, no matter which road you choose to take, you must be willing to commit, dig in for the long haul, to reap the benefits at the end. Remember, anything worthwhile is worth waiting for.

I am no different from you! I have struggled through life. Schooling, career challenges, health issues, relationship disasters, financial woes, and parenting trials are just a few of the areas where I have skinned my knees. You name it, I have faced it, and more. I truly believe that we only learn life's true lessons by living through them.

I am not attempting to give you the cure-all or the secret that others claim they can give you. There is no quick fix in life, and if someone tries to sell it to you, quickly walk or run in the opposite direction. I am going to give you something even more valuable than the quick fix. I am going to relate, in simple terms, what I have learned from some of the greatest people who I have met in my life. These are not famous or award-winning authors, scholars, doctors, or politicians, but rather just extraordinary people; people who grasp the essence of life and those who have truly lived their lives with balance. Those special people that can leave the earth and truly say that they "got it." These individuals truly found their sprinkles!

I am going to give you the biggest gift of all. A real-life formula for success, based on real-life experiences. If applied correctly, it will take you wherever you want to go. However, you must have conviction and determination. Without the drive and commitment, you will find it hard, if not impossible to achieve whatever you are searching for in life. To find what is missing, you need to be honest with yourself. There is no room for false promises or partial commitment. The process starts and ends with you.

Whether you're seeking a sense of balance in your relationships, work, financial status, spiritual being, or just simply feeling the need to go in a new direction, this book will get you there. We will explore the recipe for success. The entire book will carefully map out your personal journey while comparing it to the baking process of cupcakes. Cupcakes? Yes, the baking process of cupcakes! You see, assembling the right mixture of ingredients to foster your success in life is much like mixing and baking up a batch of cupcakes. Every stage along the way is a vital link in the process. We often try to make life difficult, more complicated than it really it is. I have news: it's not that complicated. In fact, often the answer is so simple that we can't see it.

What's really missing in your life? It's one simple ingredient, but yet the most important, the sprinkles. We Americans, quite frankly, have lost our sprinkles. The world is in a state of sprinkle depletion. Sprinkles make each individual special. Sprinkles make life exciting. Sprinkles are the ingredient that shines brightest on the darkest of days. Some may call it the human spirit. Some may call it mojo. I call it sprinkles.

DEDICATION

This book is dedicated to my parents...the two people that have taught me, not so much through words, but more so through their actions, that life is all about how you treat people. They have taught me that the way that you carry yourself and the love that you share with one another are your true stamps on life. Every day is an opportunity to spread the sprinkles. There are always points in life when you either can laugh or cry. We Motts choose to laugh. There is something infectious about a good giggle. Even if the giggle is at our own expense.

My mom, Phyllis, passed away from pancreatic cancer about ten years ago. She was a nurse for years and then went on to become the director of nursing at Children's Hospital at Stanford University in California. She was a magnificent woman. Mom was one of the most loving and intelligent women that has ever graced the planet. Despite her off-the-chart intellect, she loved to dumb it down and make fun of herself at any given opportunity. She was constantly coming up with something new and different to add a certain sprinkle to life. It was either pretending to be Mrs. Chicken outside the window to coax us into eating our eggs, or whipping up a batch of her famous Mickey Mouse waffles and asking us, "Which part are you going to eat first, the eyes, nose, or mouth?" Fun was her middle name and she was eager to volunteer her services as someone she called "Madam Ginette," an off-the-wall fortune-teller with crystal ball in tow. I can't remember which were longer, the eyelashes, fingernails, or the tales of your future which she conjured up totally off the cuff.

Despite my mother's creativity and antics, my father, Rodney, remains to this day the flamboyant one of the two. Yes, my mom had a sense of humor; however, she was humorous in an artful way. Dad just likes to get it out there. He is always very comfortable in the spotlight.

If I had to tell one story about my dad, it would be this. Early in his life, he was a lifeguard at the Jersey Shore. This was back before the spray tan. One night he and some friends were enjoying fellowship on the beach. You know, the kind of fellowship that often involves empty aluminum cans and an over-inflated sense of self-worth. On this given night, one of his buddies bet him that he couldn't swim across the Atlantic Ocean to England and back. Being the confident fellow that he was, my father decided to go for a swim. He was a lifeguard and an excellent swimmer, so he gave it the good old college try. As he reached the mile marker off shore, he was winded and the alcohol started to wear off. As the shoreline lights seemed to drift away, his senses returned, and he realized that he had done enough. He made an immediate U turn and headed back for land. As he sauntered up onto the beachhead, all of his friends were standing there waiting anxiously with concerned expressions. As my dad passed them, a bit winded, he simply said, "The Brits send their regards, now pay up!"

Needless to say my parents created the perfect blend, complementing one another at each turn and loving every minute of it. They were a walking example of how balance in your life serves to augment your sprinkles. Thanks, Mom and Dad. Love you both.

CHAPTER 1

WHAT'S BAKING AMERICA?

A re you paying attention to what's happening around you? Every five seconds, one child dies from a hunger-related cause. Do you know what's happening in America? Every nine seconds, a student becomes a dropout. When was the last time you didn't take for granted having a roof over your head? One hundred million people worldwide are homeless. What about our planet? Every thirty minutes a new species becomes extinct. We are literally trashing our planet and looking the other way. Did you know that there's a plastic trash vortex that's floating around in the middle of the ocean? It's twice the size of Texas!

Let's face it. We are a wasteful society. Every year, over 260 million tons of plastic are produced on this great planet of ours. Much of it is for one-time disposable use. The travesty is that roughly 90 percent never makes it to a proper recycling facility. So where does it end up? The answer is the vortex. We are raping and pillaging our planet. Whether you believe in global warming or not, I would hope that we would all agree that we have done a disservice to our home, planet Earth. If we don't take equal responsibility for both the problem and the solution, our legacy might just be that we wasted our opportunity for change.

This is not the time to be complacent. Most of us have decided to ignore the news because it's simply depressing. After all, it's just one dismal fact or event after another. Haven't you ever heard the expression, "Ignorance is bliss"? Bliss, in this case, will most likely be short lived. The question is, is this the best time to bury your head in the sand? Is this the time to ride through life wearing blinders? Are you willing to let ignorance dictate your fate?

As I was riding through Amish country during a recent visit to the East Coast, I was amazed to see this quiet culture that has managed to stand still for years. This gentle group of people have insulated themselves from the ever-changing effects of the world. They are constantly struggling to maintain their values and simple lifestyle. As I passed hundreds of majestic farms, through the rolling hills of Pennsylvania, it was difficult not to admire, and even envy, the beauty of it all. Silos dotted the landscape, in the midst of miles and miles of cornfields. This sight created a visual tapestry like no other. As we slowly drove the winding roads, up would pop this scene, as if we were transported back in time. Slowly trotting down the road in front of us appeared a simple horse and buggy. This is the only mode of transportation that the Amish use to travel the countryside.

Leading the charge was a majestic, retired race horse, trotting down the roadway with buggy in tow. The horse wore blinders so as not to be spooked by anything to its left or right. This majestic animal was looking forward always and concentrating only on its ultimate destination. As I recognized this fact, I couldn't help but draw the correlation between the horse and Americans these days. Don't we all have our blinders on at times? A good majority of the time, we're so focused on getting from point A to point B that we lose sight of what's happening around us.

I'm an avid runner. My set routine is to run in the morning at approximately the same time each day. I have started to recognize that the people that I pass are no different from the horse pulling the buggy. They literally have their blinders on and don't expect any contact from the left or right. Recognizing this fact, I decided to experiment with the horses (the different folks that I met on my run). Every morning, as I ventured out, I made a commitment to myself that I would reach out to everyone that crossed my path.

This was very interesting. On week one, I greeted everyone with a simple, "Good morning," "How you doing?" or even "What a loot! You're going to be a rich man!" to the homeless man that was digging through the recycling bin. I was amazed at how shocked they were as I drew them out of what I like to call "the blinder zone." If you could have seen the homeless man as he bolted out of the recycling bin. Tin cans were flying everywhere! I wish I'd had cameras rolling. His reaction was priceless! All the other encounters were equally amazing. Looks of bewilderment, disgust, terror, and unwelcome interruption were the norm.

What's this world coming to when a simple gesture of kindness raises such an eyebrow? After the results of week one, I decided to push forward with my experiment. As I hit the road, same time every morning, taking the same route every day of week two, I was meeting the same people each morning. I quickly realized that as much as I was following a routine, so were they. I could count on them being in the same spot at the same time. I expected to get the same response, or so I thought. As I showed the same level of enthusiasm, the astonishment seemed to diminish and the interaction started to pick up. I started to receive a simple wave, "hello," and/or "good morning" in return.

Week three came along, again, out at the same time, the same route, and the same folks. However, this week was different. This week was special. As I approached from fifteen yards away, they began to recognize me. They had become conditioned to a positive outcome from our interaction. It was beautiful. This is when the magic happened. From ten yards away, I noticed a simple grin. Their facial expressions started to light up. I could feel it, and I know they felt it as well. A beautiful thing originated out of a "hello" or "good morning."

I couldn't help but think about that classic scene in *How the Grinch Stole Christmas*. The Grinch had just lugged all of his loot to the highest hill and was waiting to see what the Whos' reaction would be to the fact that he had stolen Christmas. As they awakened, he heard not despair, but rather the sound of joy and singing. At that moment, he realized that Christmas was not about the material things; it was about the spirit and the kindness. At that moment, he started to grow a heart, and a simple grin grew across his face.

Much like the Grinch, there seemed to be a spirit that was rekindled in the folks with whom I had repetitive contact. This, however, was not a one-way street. As their faces brightened with that simple grin, my running pace started to pick up. I felt like a million bucks. Yes, I started it, and I was receiving in return. I paid it forward and it was paying dividends. This quest of restoring or rekindling that lost spirit is what I like to call "starting a tidal wave of sprinkles."

I had just proven that we all have our blinders on from time to time. What is more important, I had proven that whether the blinders are installed consciously or unconsciously, they are detrimental. Yes, they allow us to get from point A to point B, but in the process, we are missing out on many of the positive interactions that life has to offer. Now, let's be real. We all need to focus at times, and we can't always smell every rose along the way. However, I'm here to say that blinders have become a way of life and we need to call attention to them. For our own benefit, we must cast them away. As we make the conscious decision not to look left or right, the world is suffering. Our planet is baking.

We can all remember pivotal times in our lives; times when something so horrible changed us and, at the same time, ignited a passion within that forced a certain action. For those who are from an older generation, it might be the attack on Pearl Harbor or the Holocaust. These were pivotal points that were so devastating, they forced America and the world to stand up and say, "Enough is enough." For the current generation, it might be that fateful day when planes started flying into buildings. If you think back, I bet you can remember exactly where you were and what you were doing at that moment. Time stood still. This single act seemed to reboot America and the world. The date 9/11 will forever be seen as the day that America threw away its blinders. On that fateful day we realized that we were not exempt from the forces of evil. On that single day, and in the midst of extreme tragedy, people across America found their inner strength. They realized in a split second what mattered in the world. It was kindness. In a blink of an eye, we regained our vision. As a very wise blind woman once said, "We are never really happy until we try to brighten the lives of others." This wise blind woman was Helen Keller. Helen was both blind and deaf from birth. How-

4

ever, she lived life with great clarity and vision. Life tried to force her to live with blinders, but she pushed way beyond her handicap.

Today should be considered our next 9/11. Our core temperature is rising. Everyone in America and the world is baking. If action is not taken immediately, tragedy is inevitable. We are depleting everything within ourselves and around us. If we don't remove our heads from the sand, if we don't rip the blinders off, we might as well grab the controls to the plane and fly it into the building. I understand that's a strong statement. However, destructive things are happening all around us. The polar ice caps are shrinking at an alarming rate. The waste that our children will inherit is expanding like no other. Let's face it. Everyone on this planet is about the quick fix. Whether it's for food or energy, we are opting for the artificial choice. All of our actions are based around taking, consuming, and using all the natural resources within the world. We are literally taking without giving back. In return, the earth's temperature is on the rise. I have news. If the planet is sick, we might as well be.

If we don't stand up today and put our foot down, we may find ourselves past the point of no return. For those of you who are riding through life thinking, "It will just work itself out," it will surely not. It's time for all of us in the world to step up and take responsibility. It's time for us to step up and own the situation. It's time for us all to crawl out of the shadow of the worldly recession and display again the true traits of the human spirit. The resurrection of our society and the preservation of the planet are in the hands of each one of us. Just as we have the power to create evil acts that stir the world, we have the power to create simple, but amazing acts that rekindle the sprinkles within. These single acts can start a tidal wave of goodwill.

"You must be the change you wish to see in the world."—Mahatma Gandhi

CHAPTER 2

WHAT ARE YOU CRAVING?

I s there something missing in your life? Are you bogged down in the same old routine and wish you could break loose? What do you want to be when you grow up, or have you actually forgotten or lost sight of what it was? Is your most intimate relationship lacking in some way? Is there never enough time for what's really important in life? Is all of your time spent on meaningless activities that don't enrich your life? Are you lacking in love, friendship, wealth, money, or all the above? Have you built a machine around you that only sucks the energy and life force out of you while giving little back in return?

No matter what the question, the missing element, the obstacle, or the direction that you wish to go in, it's imperative that you understand what drives you. For every real desire, there is an equally compelling will to accomplish it. You need to be honest with yourself and identify what you crave in life. You must identify if the cravings are healthy or unhealthy. Above all, you need to identify your true passion. *Passion in life is like super unleaded gasoline. It's the best stuff to put into your tank if you desire the utmost in performance.* Achieve a higher level of performance in life and I guarantee your thirst will be quenched for anything you crave.

Once you have identified what you are lacking, searching for, or craving in life, it's easy to find the motivation to make it happen. If there's an unhealthy craving, identification will lead you to properly handle it. It will steer you away from things that hurt and hinder. On the other hand, other cravings that don't necessarily hurt can, in turn, drive you to accomplish goals that you wouldn't normally try to achieve. For instance, my girlfriend and I were driving down the road one day and this young man came running past us. He was in his midtwenties, had his shirt off, and looked like a Greek god! I mean, he was chiseled! As he passed us, I quickly noticed my girlfriend's reaction, as her neck seemed to turn with him. Seriously, if her head wasn't attached to her body, it would have been down the street chasing after this guy. Yes, I have to admit, this guy was a head turner. As my girlfriend's head was contorting in ways that I never knew were possible, I was picking her jaw up off the ground at the same time. At that moment, I realized that her reaction was something that I desired for myself; something that I craved.

Now, don't take this the wrong way. My girlfriend loves me and, for the sake of a good read, I may have gone overboard describing her reaction. However, in the end, the point is still the same. My girlfriend loves me no matter what the circumstance. She has proven this fact day after day as I have embarked on this journey to reboot. Going from three thousand square feet with all the creature comforts to barely two hundred is not without its sacrifices. It takes an understanding woman and a whole lot of unconditional love to weather those kind of life changes without threatening to abandon ship. This is exactly why she is my best friend in life.

The question wasn't whether she loved me or would stand by me. Rather, the question was, did she have the same feeling when she looked at me with my shirt off as she did with the Greek god that just trotted by us? I can hear the critics as I write this. What a shallow desire. She should love you for who you are and not what she desires you to be. Don't be so quick to condemn her for being herself. For goodness' sake, as I said before, she puts up with my crazy three teenagers and my father, who acts like a teenager. Placing that aside, it's not shallow to be drawn to attractive things, and that was merely what she was doing. It was nothing more than enjoying the scenery. I once heard someone say, "I don't care where you get your appetite, just as long as you come home to eat with me." Life is a beautiful place, people included.

If I'm honest, I will admit that there are highs and lows in our relationship. At that moment, there was something missing; just that little added sprinkle of excitement. Haven't you ever become comfortable in a relationship and taken things for granted? Yes, we all do. Why does this happen? This happens as a result of easing off the gas pedal. There are peaks and valleys to every relationship. In the valleys we tend not to expend the same amount of energy as we do climbing the hills of the courting or dating process. Just as a car uses more gasoline to conquer an incline, so do we as we come across the same in relationships. It's natural for us to seize the opportunity to coast a bit. Whether you admit it or not, you lose major momentum quickly by coasting along in the flat sections. The only time that this doesn't happen is in the downhill sections. During the downhills, momentum is gained quickly. We can easily take our foot off the gas and coast a bit as life's gravity is working with us. We often find ourselves having to hold back in these sections as the road can often be extremely treacherous.

It's interesting how we go from making sure every aspect of our appearance is just right for the first date to just throwing on a T-shirt and barely shaving three months into the relationship. We tend to rest on our laurels and just assume that the flame will keep burning at the same intensity. We back off on the sprinkles. We start to coast.

I'm here to tell you, *all flames need oxygen to exist. Cut off the oxygen and the flame is sure to go out.* When I saw my girlfriend's reaction to the guy running, it immediately ignited a fire from within. It was like someone flipped a switch. Some voice inside said, "I want that!" Then I asked myself, "What is stopping me from attaining the same reaction?" I realized that the biggest obstacle was my inner voice. It was saying, "Old guys can't look like that! You won't be able to stick to it! You can't do it." Instead of subscribing to the "can't" philosophy, it was time to obliterate the *t*. It was time to proclaim to the universe, "Yes, I can, and I will."

Now we all know that this doesn't just apply to one's love life. It applies to every relationship that surrounds us. *The demise of any relationship is taking things for granted.* All relationships require constant effort and work. Whether it's in the workplace, in the family, with God, or anyone else, *if you choose not to water it, it will cease to grow and flourish.*

I chose that day to start fanning the flames. I started running. Was it an easy process? No, but I was committed! Some have said that change is not an event, but rather a process. I agree on one hand, but on the other I disagree. *With any true change, there needs to be a life-changing event, an awakening.* One moment that ignites the fire from within. It's the single moment that becomes the catalyst for the process. Is this the time and place for you? You can make it happen today! You too can find your sprinkles!

My catalyst was the encounter with the runner and the reaction from my girlfriend. It called attention to my desire and in turn ignited my will. From that point on, I clearly identified with what I was craving in that aspect of my life. I decided to set in motion a certain plan to achieve my goal. I always say, *"Purpose along with commitment equates to a mission!"* Within days, I set out on a mission and saw immediate positive results. Yes, it took hard work, conviction, and dedication, but as a result, my girlfriend started to see me through a different set of eyes. As I was dropping in weight, she stated that she felt like she was having an affair with a new man. The transformation was not only physical but mental as well. My self-confidence was up and, in turn, people noticed. I'm a firm believer in the following: *If you want to effect positive mental changes in your life, your body needs to lead the way. It's so difficult to be mentally strong in this world if your body is sending you negative messages.* As a result of these positive physical and mental changes, there were amazing accomplishments that accompanied them.

This wish to become fit was a long-term desire; one that would take me some time to accomplish. It's imperative for you to understand what's involved so you can identify what it will take to accomplish your goals. On the flip side, it's just as important to be able to identify your short-term urges that can derail you from your long-term pursuit. Short-term physical urges are often your body's way of saying that you have depleted something essential within yourself. With becoming fit, my short-term cravings to eat were standing in the way of reaching my goal. When we fail to pay attention and simply try to satisfy the craving, we tend to reach in the wrong direction without thinking. This wrong direction might seem like such a simple and harmless act. However, the simplest of things can end up being the catalyst for negative changes in your life. Habits both positive and negative are started in the same single second. Simple or complex, they both can have an impact on your life in a major way.

It's imperative that you recognize the following potential eating pitfalls. I refer to them as the C4s of cravings. For those of you who are unfamiliar with C4, it's a common term for plastic explosive. C4 has many advantages. It's easily molded into any shape. It's one of the most flexible of all explosives. Due to its flexibility, it's often invisible to the naked eye. However, just as it has its advantages, it's equally destructive. The C4s of cravings are attractive for their quick fix. They are often invisible to the naked eye and can be destructive when it comes to our pursuit of a well-balanced and successful lifestyle. They are as follows:

C_1 = Chocolate. Chocolate is one of my personal vices and just happens to be one of the most widely craved foods in America. As a young child, I dreamed of being Charlie, finding the golden ticket and having a run at the chocolate factory. Imagine it, all the chocolate you ever wanted. Is our desire to consume chocolate all Willy Wonka's fault, or is there something more that our bodies crave? The answer is no to Wonka and yes to the deeper craving. Two of chocolate's key ingredients are directly linked to why we crave it so much. Chocolate contains phenylethylamine (PEA), which regulates the body's release of endorphins, and also contains traces of tetrahydrocannabinol (THC), a substance found in marijuana. So, in other words, you are consuming ingredients that reduce feelings of stress and, in turn, set you off on a self-induced high. What could possibly be better in life? I don't have a care in the world and I feel like I can accomplish anything. The only problem is that it's artificial and a short-term fix. Remember, what goes up in life must come down. In this case, a chocolate high is one without a parachute. Along with these mood-lifting ingredients, chocolate is also high in iron content. Iron is one of the key minerals that are depleted in women during their menstrual periods. Earth-shattering news…roses and chocolate are not really the way to a woman's heart, but rather the cure for her iron deficiency. Who would have guessed it?

This point is critical to understand. Just as the runner and my girlfriend's reaction to him ignited a spark within me, so too can your body send signals to your brain to seek out what it's craving. Rarely do your mind and your body have the conversation in front of you. They are sneaky players in life. They often have back-door conversations and you're not invited to the party. They are very persistent and won't let up on their assault to get what they want until they are completely satisfied. If there is no thought to analyze why your body is singing a certain tune, you will automatically jump in with the chorus. The downside is, your body's urges and its cravings are not always in your best interest. Can you imagine what your body would look like if you ate chocolate every time you had a craving? Can you imagine the negative effects on your mind and spirit if you simply went about life satisfying your every desire? At this moment, I am simply talking about chocolate. However, there are things that we are attracted to in life other than just food. Cravings can be both good and bad. Just as they can set you off in a positive direction, they can derail you just as fast. So pay attention to what your mind and body are telling you and ask yourself if they are truly acting in your best interest.

C_2 = Chips. Potato chips are a major vice, but in reality it's the salt that people really crave. A craving for salt normally means that you have taken your body to a point where it's dehydrated. Dehydration is the process by which your body loses water, electrolytes, and salt. Athletes are constantly struggling with this battle as they tend to lose these ingredients through intense or extended exercise. The best way to fight dehydration is by drinking more water and by replacing the lost salt. Many sports drinks provide the necessary nutrients for hydration, especially after an intense workout. Thirst in life can be a very strong and motivating force. However, thirst is not simply created by the lack of salt. Thirst can be created when you're lacking in any area. Love, companionship, money, warmth, and the list is continuous. If you are deprived in any of the areas mentioned above, there will be a thirst that is created and thus a desire to quench it. Imagine the following scenario: You are lost in the desert. Your thirst level is at an all-time high. Your senses are starting to get the best of you. At this point any liquid will do. You stumble upon an oasis of vodka and start consuming. Alcohol only serves to dehydrate you more. Your initial thirst might be quenched. However, your state of dehydration has only worsened. This is a prime example of how an immediate fix in a state of deprivation, may not always be the best solution. I liken it to going grocery shopping on an empty stomach. Not a good idea.

C_3 = Carbohydrates. Carbohydrate cravings often occur in the midafternoon, when your energy stores are at their lowest. I personally get them around two to three o'clock. After sitting in front of a computer screen and or talking on the phone all day, I constantly have to fight the urge to go down to the community kitchen for a quick vending snack. News flash! *Nothing good ever comes out of a vending machine unless it's water.* The healthy alternative to unhealthy snacking would be to eat a handful of nuts, dried fruit, or yogurt to give you the energy you need. These will provide you with healthy proteins and carbohydrates that will satisfy your cravings. Your energy levels will be restored to normal and your productivity will increase. Bottom line, your body needs energy. Carbohydrates supply that energy. Reach for the right carbohydrates.

C_4 = Caffeine. Caffeine is the deadliest component of the C_4 equation. I say it's the deadliest, as I truly believe that it comes from the dark side. It's the voice of the devil when it comes to our urge for the quick fix. Our culture is conditioned to search out and consume caffeine in large amounts. Often our days start and end with consuming this very addictive substance. If you're tired, it's either a cup of coffee, an energy drink, or some miracle in a packet that promises you a certain amount of energy. Caffeine is as addictive as some drugs out there. One dose leads to another and so on. Before you know it, you are constantly searching out a caffeine fix to stimulate activity in the brain. After the dose of caffeine wears off, it often creates a craving for additional caffeine. Have you ever heard constant coffee drinkers say that they get headaches when they try to cut down on their caffeine consumption? If not, believe me, it happens. Caffeine, the pusher, has hooked the individual, hook, line, and sinker. When the person eventually realizes that he or she is dependent on caffeine and tries to break away, the body and the brain send a signal that it's not okay, thus the headache. This is your body's way of signaling that it needs more.

More often than not, you are not consuming just the item with caffeine. For you folks who can't live without that cup of coffee, it's normally just the first in a string of very bad decisions throughout the day. For starters, the cup of coffee is usually accompanied by a doughnut or an unhealthy snack. It may also be replacing that morning workout. It's imperative that you see caffeine as the ring leader. You must dethrone him right away! Caffeine is like the drug pusher who wants to suck you in, get you addicted, and once he does, he has you forever. Once you start things off on the wrong foot, one bad decision leads to another. Before you know it, the day is blown and you are looking toward tomorrow to start on the right track. *In life, there are no guarantees that tomorrow will exist, so why not live the right way today?*

If you are fatigued throughout the day, there are healthier choices then reaching for any one of the C4s. First, make sure you are getting enough sleep! Without the proper amount of sleep, your ability to reason with cravings is severely compromised. Second, exercise daily. Most of us think that we will be more tired by exercising. It's the opposite. Exercise has been proven to increase your energy levels and enable you to overcome food cravings. For those of us that have hit forty, the truth is this: when you wake up, you are going to be sore whether you've exercised or not. It takes more for your body to get going in the morning as you grow older. The question is no longer "To be sore or not to be?" as it's going to happen either way. If it's inevitable, you might as well enjoy the positive effects that accompany exercise versus the negative effects of living a sedentary, sore lifestyle.

The true question is, who do you really want to be? Do you want to be the person who is governed by unsophisticated urges, cravings, or the one who keeps them at bay to stay the course? Are you that person that turns your cravings into motivation and, in turn, momentum? What do you want to mix up in life and broadcast to the universe? Do you want to mix up a batch of chocolate or vanilla cupcakes? Which are you now, and is that who you really want to be? Are you a Will Be, Wanna Be, Wish Be, Won't Be, or a Wah Wah Be? Let's examine them a bit.

Will Be—the eternal optimist. The "Will Bes" only know "can." They despise the word "can't," so the letter *t* is not included in their vocabulary. They have a clear-cut vision regarding what they want in life. They have drive that goes one way, the right way. They can be knocked down and they truly believe that getting back up is just another step in the journey to success. They are the people to be around, and good things seem to seek them out at every turn. Their positive attitude is contagious.

Wanna Be—the person that must be included. The "Wanna Be" is the person who constantly wants to be on the "in." They live to be accepted by those around them and will jump on any train as long as everyone else is on it. They lack self-identity, as all their traits are borrowed from those around them. These individuals are rarely satisfied, as they constantly want more than they will ever have in life.

Wish Be—the ever-so-popular dreamer. The "Wish Be" is always wishing for more and never quite content with the present. This person shares many of the traits of the Wanna Be. This person has high aspirations and will even go as far as planning out how to achieve them. The Wish Bes shortcoming is that he or she is easily excited about the new idea but quickly loses interest when challenged with what it takes to achieve it. He or she rarely acts on the grand plan. He or she is constantly coming up with great ideas and wishing that they could come true. These individuals will most likely be avid lottery players. They are often jealous of those that they perceive to have more in life. Often more than not, they make constant excuses why they have not achieved their dreams.

Won't Be—the eternal pessimist. The "Won't Bes" are the devil's best friends, as they are always singing the tune of discouragement. "It will never work." "It won't ever happen." "I can't do this." "You can't accomplish that." The cup is definitely half empty with this type of individual. This individual never takes any accountability for his or her own actions. It's always him or her against the world, and the world is winning the fight. This individual preys on the weak minded, as they are easy recruits when it comes to getting others to jump on the doom-and-gloom bandwagon.

Wah Wah Be—the ultimate complainer. The "Wah Wah Be" may be on board, but he or she is griping about it with every step. It's always too hot, too cold, never just right. These people are like nails on the chalkboard when trying to coexist with the Wish Bes and the Will Bes. They get along with Won't Bes, as they feed off their negativity. These individuals were taught at an early age that if you cry loud enough or complain long enough, you will be given attention. They normally lack attention from those that they care about the most and are using the wrong vehicle in an attempt to capture it.

So the question is…what do you want in life? What are you craving? Who are you now and who do you really want to be? Are you the type of person that can identify your long-term cravings and harness your inner strength to achieve what you want in life? Are you able to control your short-term cravings to protect yourself from the evils of the world that are sure to send you into a tailspin? Is there room for personal growth in this stage of the baking process? What type or flavor of individual do you want to be in life?

Mott-Ohs

Passion in life is like super unleaded gasoline. It's the best stuff to put into your tank if you desire the utmost in performance.

All flames need oxygen to exist. Cut off the oxygen and the flame is sure to go out.

The demise of any relationship is taking things for granted.

If you choose not to water it, it will cease to grow and flourish.

With any true change, there needs to be a life-changing event.

Purpose along with commitment equates to a mission!

If you want to effect positive mental changes in your life, your body needs to lead the way. It is so difficult to be mentally strong in this world if your body is sending you negative messages.

Nothing good ever comes out of a vending machine unless it's water.

In life, there are no guarantees that tomorrow will exist, so why not live the right way today?

CHAPTER 3

IS YOUR KITCHEN A MESS?

I s your kitchen a mess? Do you lack the tools to accomplish your priorities or goals in life? Are you constantly going around in circles, spinning your wheels, and going nowhere fast?

Have you ever walked into someone's kitchen and on the surface it looks spotless? As you dig deeper, you suddenly realize that behind the facade, there's chaos in the kitchen. The pantry is a mess. It's unorganized. Dated and expired products litter the shelves. As you open drawers, does a clutter monster, threatening to eat you alive, jump out at you? Now, admit it. How many of you have these drawers? These are the drawers that are capable of swallowing anything. Oh, there's my third child! I have been looking for him everywhere. Where has he been? The catchall drawer! How can anyone function like this? How many areas of your life mirror these drawers? Does this kitchen of chaos sound much like your life? What if I was to suggest that you are only as good as your most unorganized drawer? Scary thought, isn't it?

When you were younger, your parents told you to clean your room and then told you the same thing again. You probably assumed that it was their fate to nag at you. They were trying to teach you a valuable lesson. This lesson consisted of one simple premise: *If you want to ultimately be successful, you must be highly organized.* Being organized reduces your frustration in life by increasing your efficiency. *You can't be searching for matching socks all your life. On the same note, throw away all the worn socks, or the ones that have holes! It's like unloading life's old baggage.*

Just as we size up people's kitchens, we also form perceptions of people, only to find out later that they are nothing like our initial assessment. They are full of cluttered drawers, expired and outdated products, and lacking the tools to reach and achieve their true potential. Their kitchen is often a mess. Why do we do this? It's because we form most of our opinions of others based on that first impression; all we see is the door to the kitchen or pantry. It literally takes seconds to form a first impression. It's important to realize that first impressions can be both a good scale and a deceiving one. Due to the deceiving end, *I am a firm believer that the truth is not found consistently at the front door but rather behind it.*

My father once told me that he sized everyone up instantly by the shoes that they were wearing. This is an interesting idea. It makes much sense. With men's shoes especially, it takes some effort to keep them looking in tip-top shape. I respect the power of the first impression. For that reason, you can count on finding me at the shoeshine stand whenever I am flying somewhere for business. I learned very early on in life that *you never get a second chance to make a first impression. You have but one chance to shine.*

If the shoes are shiny, well polished, and in good shape, the initial perception would be that the individual was conscientious and had his or her act together. If the shoes were in disrepair, lacking that sparkly finish, and overall detracting from that first impression, the chances are the other details of the person's life are handled in the same fashion. The impression would be that the person was not organized, lacked attention to detail, and was not so on top of his or her game. Using shoes is simply a trick to get a peek at the inside of someone's inner pantry. So I ask you: How do your shoes look? And more importantly, how is the ground beneath you, as it serves as the foundation for all things to come?

Now that we have identified that our kitchens must be in order and well equipped inside and out, it's imperative for all of us to break our kitchen down and recognize where it is lacking. Have you ever walked into your kitchen only to find a disaster area? You immediately ask yourself, how did it get this way? This happens very often in life. We find ourselves in a situation or a state of disrepair and have no idea how we sank so low. One day you wake up and you're twenty pounds heavier than you think you should be. One day you wake up and you're twenty thousand dollars in debt. One day you wake up and twenty years have passed and you have little to nothing to show for it. How did I get to this point? This is what I call a CNL, a compound negative landslide. Much like a landslide, there is normally one single catalyst that starts the entire slide; one rock that triggers a negative chain reaction that ultimately ends in disaster. To understand the landslide fully, it's imperative to pinpoint the catalyst. A catalyst can easily be defined as a person, thing, or event that starts a certain chain of events. Anything short of identifying the catalyst will only lead to further landslides or a short-term fix.

Allow me to draw the following analogy. Have you ever been speeding down the road, everything is fine, and all of sudden, clunk! Your car hits a pothole.

It's an entire blowout. The blowout is just the collateral damage from the pothole. The true question is, where do your potholes lie in life, and how did they get there in first place? It's important to understand the anatomy of a pothole. Potholes are created from small cracks in the road surface. Water penetrates the crack and travels down to the foundation and compromises the overall strength of the roadway. Once this compromised state meets the weight of a car tire, the road starts to fail and the pothole is formed. Our personal foundation must be in good repair at all times. If there is a state of disrepair, the foundation is sure to crumble under the stress that life has to offer.

As you are walking down the street, take notice of the cracks in the asphalt. Then start searching for where the road workers have made temporary patches. If you find the older temporary patches, you will soon realize that the cracks are coming back. These cracks aren't coming back in the patch itself. They reach out from the edges even farther than where they were initially. Why is this? Because when the technicians patched the initial crack, they did nothing to correct the real problem. The real problem was much deeper. The real problem was lying in the foundation of the roadway. What started with a simple crack in the asphalt soon became a deeper problem when left in disrepair. Time and life's elements had exploited the weakness of the crack and had traveled down to the foundation. They had eaten away at the base material that supported the roadway. Therefore, *you must identify the deeper problem that exists beneath your surface cracks.* You must repair the cracks before they develop into bigger problems.

It's similar to walking into the kitchen and smelling a rancid odor. You immediately grab the air freshener and the problem goes away. But the problem goes away just for the moment, only to shortly return. You then find some rotting vegetables in the fridge. *You must find the source and correct it before moving forward.*

Ten years ago, I was freshly divorced and I was mad. I wasn't dealing with my problems. I was too busy feeling sorry for myself. Instead of dealing with my surface cracks, I allowed them to fester into huge problems in my foundation. I made a bad decision to numb my feelings with alcohol. Yes, the alcohol eased my pain temporarily, but in the end, it was like placing a Band-Aid on a bullet wound. I thought I was in total control by making the decision to be mad. The anger, along with the alcohol, was just covering up the real work that needed to be done. It wasn't until two years into my postdivorce period that I got down to the real work: the repair process. I decided to rip the Band-Aid off and expose the bullet wound. I identified what I was mad about, straightened up the messy drawers, and put my kitchen back in order. Once I identified the messy areas of my life, I made the very conscious decision that being mad was an absolute waste of time and was counterproductive. I decided to stop drowning my feelings in alcohol and met them head on. Once I exposed the real issues, life started shooting forward in all sorts of different positive directions.

Are there deeper problems with your kids that you fail to recognize? What is happening at work that's making you miserable? Why is there never enough money? Why is time not on your side? Why is your marriage not as fulfilling as you would like it to be? Why are you constantly struggling with your weight? Once you identify these areas and then dig deeper into the foundation, you are well on your way to fixing the situation. *Acceptance and being honest about the current state of your kitchen is half the battle.*

Once you start attacking the root problems, you will quickly see that the repair has far-reaching, positive effects. For instance, when I started running, my health started to improve. When my health started to improve, my energy level went way up. When my energy level went up, my productivity in work, play, and all other facets of life started to improve. *Once you start improving just the smallest areas that lead to the deepest cracks, you will see a measurable effect.* Regardless of the problems that may exist, it's best that you identify the worst and start with the biggest priorities first.

I have been a coffee drinker for quite some time. I have never been the type of coffee drinker that absolutely has to have that first cup to get me started. You know these people. My girlfriend is one of them. The unspoken word is, "If you even so much as look at me with your obnoxious, I-want-to-attack-the-morning look before I have my first cup, you are as good as dead where you stand!" For me, that cup of coffee is comfort food. Others truly believe that their morning coffee can make or break the day.

I must admit, I was not always an experienced coffee drinker. I remember the first time that I stepped into Starbucks, I wished that the shop came with an instruction manual. My wife, at the time, sent me to fetch a cup of coffee and carefully spelled out the details on a yellow sticky note. To this day, I can remember going into the coffee shop, sticky note in hand. As I struggled to convey the order, I was mystified by the fact that coffee could be so complicated. Fast-forward six months and "Vente Peppermint Mocha Extra Hot and Heavy on the Whip!" was literally rolling off of my tongue. I was being sucked into what I call the morning vortex. What started with a sticky note soon became a morning routine: a souped-up coffee on steroids, soon to be followed with an egg, bacon, and cheese breakfast sandwich. I should have known to stay away from sticky notes. If you think about it, sticky notes adhere to everything. As much as they might remind you of things to do, they also serve to clutter your life. They are a wasteful tool and bad for the environment. If I had just avoided that initial sticky note, I wouldn't be sitting here questioning myself. "How did I get to be 215 pounds? How did I gain forty-five pounds from my high school weight?" At the time of my twenty-year high school reunion, using simple math, that's an average weight gain of two pounds per year. Was it the morning vortex or was it the compound negative landslide that I introduced earlier in this chapter—an eventual landslide that originated from a single, simple event?

Just as we choose to make good decisions and repair areas of our kitchen, we can easily make bad ones that have far-reaching effects. What started with what I thought was a simple trip to the coffee shop for a much-needed energy boost quickly turned into an energy drain. It sucked money out of my pocket to the tune of ten dollars per day and had the absolute reverse effect on my energy level. I started my day with an immense amount of unneeded calories and comfort food that, in the long run, made me tired. My productivity at work diminished. My health suffered and, like a pebble thrown into a pond, the ripples continued to spread further and further with time. *I was defeated by a Vente Mocha!*

Just as I have identified the compound negative landslide, there is also the CPA, compound positive ascent. As easily as we choose to take a negative direction in life, we can make the conscious decision to take a positive one.

As of the writing of this chapter, I have not had a cup of coffee in forty-five days. Now most of you are saying, "No way! Not me!" Listen! Don't throw the book away! I am not saying that you have to stop and change everything. I am simply saying, *"Open your eyes and realize that the simplest of decisions can have a domino effect."*

Do I miss my morning coffee? Yes, sometimes, mostly because I liked going up to the girls at the counter and saying, "Extra hot and heavy on the whip!" with a little shit-ass grin on my face. However, the long-term benefits outweigh the short-term gratification. I am feeling way better. My energy level is up, and there are ten more dollars in my pocket every day. I chose to create a CPA rather than a CNL. I chose to make the conscious decision and clean up my kitchen. *Make the right decision to repair the deficient areas of your life, and the effects will be far reaching.*

Mott-Ohs

If you want to ultimately be successful, you must be highly organized.

You can't be searching for matching socks all your life. On the same note, throw away all the worn socks, or the ones that have holes! It's like unloading life's old baggage.

I am a firm believer that the truth is not found consistently at the front door, but rather behind it.

You never get a second chance to make a first impression. You have but one chance to shine.

You must identify the deeper problem that exists beneath your surface cracks.

You must find the source and correct it before moving forward.

Acceptance and being honest about the current state of your kitchen is half the battle.

Once you start improving just the smallest areas that lead to the deepest cracks, you will see a measurable effect.

Just as we choose to make good decisions and repair areas of our kitchen, we can easily make bad ones that have far-reaching effects.

I was defeated by a Vente Mocha!

Make the right decision to repair the deficient areas of your life and the effects will be far reaching.

CHAPTER 4

IT'S YOUR KITCHEN, YOUR CHOICE

Sometimes to make things anew involves a complete remodel. Sometimes it's necessary to rip things down to the studs and start from scratch. For those of you that have ever been through a makeover or a house remodel, you will agree that remodeling your kitchen or your home can be one of the most stressful times. It can serve as a wedge, coming between the strongest of relationships. This idea in the written word may sound extremely silly. How could something as trivial as a kitchen remodel come between people? Contemplate the idea for a while, and it's sure to become clear. The kitchen serves as the foundation for most homes. It's the heart of activity and literally feeds the household. It's where we often begin and end the day. It's one of the most popular spots in a house to congregate in fellowship. Just this past Thanksgiving, we were visiting my sister's home for the holiday. She was remarking that the house was so big, yet everyone seemed to congregate in the kitchen. It's the hub of activity. *Start to disturb the foundation, mess with the nucleus, or shake the center for nutrition and harmony, and it's sure to jostle any relationship mojo.* People are very predictable. Most of us like to have certain things exactly where we can find them with ease. Life needs to be in order. Turn the order upside down and it's sure to cause consternation.

Every person has a set of morals. Morals are core principles or values that one holds near and dear to one's heart. They are life's building blocks that distinguish right from wrong. They are the black and they are the white. There is very rarely any gray area when it comes to our established and accepted morals unless we muddy the waters as a result of waivering in life. *Our morals stand tall, lighting the way as a lighthouse does, guiding a wayward ship through the foggiest of nights.* Our morals make up our foundation. They are the glue that keeps our kitchens together.

Morals originate from our kitchen of the soul. The kitchen of the soul bakes these core principles. As they reach the ultimate temperature, they become perfectly refined ideas intertwined with our DNA. Many of these core principles have been baked before and are proven principles handed down from generation to generation. Others are born or baked up as a result of life lessons. It's imperative that we identify our morals early on in life. We must declare them to the universe and make a commitment to ourselves to hold true to them at every turn. Turn your back on them, choose to compromise their integrity, or fail to come to their defense, and the universe is sure to spin.

Throughout this book, there's an immense amount of discussion concerning the proper ingredients and foundation needed to foster success. Morals help to build that foundation for us to fall back on in life. You can have all the ingredients in the world. You can go out and spend money for a well-equipped kitchen; however, it boils down to one word. One word is the single key to unlocking your personal success combination. That word is "choice." *It's your kitchen, your choice.* I suppose, other than the word "sprinkles," the word "choice" might just be the most powerful word in this book. It's your choice when it comes to building the foundation. It's your choice to adopt the morals that will serve as your guiding light in life. It's your choice to be who you want to be. It's your choice to push or to pull. It's your choice to grab the brass ring or not. The word "choice" might just be one of the most powerful words on the planet. After all, people have died fighting for the freedom of choice and have stood up and been incarcerated over the right to choose.

Whether it's the United States Congress debating and setting into place laws—laws that protect a woman's fundamental right to choose to bear a child, to terminate a pregnancy—or the Constitution detailing individual rights to vote, the subject of choice is and will remain the most volatile, highly contested idea until the end of time. Despite the deep-seated history surrounding this subject, I still believe that most of us take this privilege for granted. For example, I was writing this page of the book while sitting in a favorite breakfast spot of mine. As I was sending out e-mails after I was laid off, I had written a note asking for advice from a close and very respected friend of mine. Contained in the note, I wrote the following sentence: "For the first time in thirty years, I am officially a free agent." After writing the sentence, I immediately had one of those eye-opening moments. We all have them. They are life's way of saying, aha! The idea hits you like a ton of bricks. I tend to call them Mott-Ohs! Mottos are maxims adopted as an expression of the guiding principle of a person. In my world, *once the aha happens and you decide to adopt these principles, they then become words to live by...Mott-Ohs!* In this case, the Mott-Oh would be, we're clearly in charge of our own destiny. It's our choice from the time that we wake up in the morning to when we rest our head at night.

Before having my epiphany in the breakfast joint, I clearly had been looking at the idea in a skewed fashion. In my mind, even though I had made the conscious decision to dive into my adopted profession, I was of the mind-set that I was owned by and worked for a higher power. Wrong! This was the wrong mind-set. I had shifted the power of choice over to my employer, when I was actually a free agent all along. I was free to come and go as I pleased. Every morning when I woke up, my feet would hit the floor, and I made the decision to work or not to work. I was in total control. Nobody was holding a gun to my head.

Many of you would make the argument that we must work to support our lifestyle. We must make an income to feed, clothe, and shelter ourselves. Yes, I agree, but in most cases we build our own dungeon of pressure. There is no reason that you need to drive a Mercedes. There is no reason that you have to wear a five-hundred-dollar pair of shoes. There is no reason that you must have a mortgage payment that's more than most people make in a month. After all, when most of us came out of college, we were making squat. I can remember my first day out of Penn State. I was like fresh meat in the job market. I launched out of school with a communications degree and an emphasis in film and video production. Yes, that meant that I had no idea of what I wanted to be in life or what I wanted to do. I was one of the many who just picked a major, drank my way through college, and was leaving it up to the universe to decide the rest of my destiny. Little did I know, it wasn't up to the universe. It was up to me. It was my kitchen, my choice. I walked out of college with a diploma and the shirt on my back. How ever did I survive? I survived on a minimalist mind-set. Why? Because in my head, I was convinced that I didn't need any more than the bare necessities. Anything after that would be sprinkles on top of the cupcake.

I can remember interviewing for my first property management job. It was a great opportunity. I didn't know it at the time, however, that one interview would spring me into a career that would span twenty years. We often underestimate the power of a single moment. However, as I look back, I thank God for that single opportunity. It set me on a job course that I wouldn't replace for the world. It was a job as an apartment manager for twelve apartments. In the scheme of things, it was small, as I am presently accustomed to managing ten thousand units at a time. The job was simple. I was to work full time. In return, I received a discount off a studio apartment. I can hear the gentleman interviewing me as clear as if it was yesterday. "Can you fix things?" My reply was, "Yes, of course!" Now for those of you that knew me then, this was a comical statement. Back then, I had no mechanical ability. Yes, I stretched the truth, but in my mind it wasn't a total farce, as I figured with some help from Home Depot, I could probably fix anything. Amazingly enough, he gave me the job. After he offered, I chose to take the job, as it was my choice.

So away I went. I moved into a four-hundred-square-foot apartment with my wife. Both the couch and stove were pullouts. To this day, I have only ever seen one stove that pulled out to save space. Regardless of how efficient it was, we were comfortable. We simply ate what we killed and didn't stretch it beyond. The mind-set was to be happy with whatever life presented. Life quickly served up my first opportunity to repair something. A resident that lived in the building came over to say that his garbage disposal had stopped working. I went to take a look. I turned on the switch and there was no sound. I pushed the reset button and determined that it needed to be replaced. I said it with confidence just to assure the resident that I knew what I was doing. Little did he know, I had no idea what I was doing. I then scheduled a follow-up appointment to replace the garbage disposal and made sure that the resident was going to be at work. This was essential, as I didn't want the resident to be watching while I read the installation instructions. After a short motivational speech from the plumbing expert at Home Depot, I decided to tackle the task. I think the process took me four hours to accomplish. After I finished, it started leaking, as I had not tightened down the fittings enough. Eventually I got it. What took me four hours to accomplish on my first try, I later learned to accomplish in less than a half hour. Two years later, I won first prize for the fastest garbage disposal installation at a trade show. This just goes to show that putting your mind to something and believing can make anything possible. It was my kitchen, my choice.

Yes, that first opportunity was a very simple way of life. We were very content; however, I was on a mission—a mission to prove myself at every turn and show the world that I was successful. It's only when we drive for more and choose to start to build what I call "The Machine" that we feel the stress of trying to maintain it. The Machine is our desired lifestyle. Most of us would agree that The Machine grows with every turn and the stress compounds right along with it. We acquire things, boats, cars, and then the ultimate money sucker, children. All of these cost money, but there is no other like the College Machine. I had no idea. Either that or I was in denial. After all, I was after the so-called American Dream and I didn't care what it was going to cost. I suppose this was my first conscious decision to buy now and pay later. It was a decision that led to a pattern: a pattern that would ultimately bring me full circle to my current lifestyle—today's lifestyle, which is extremely efficient. Again, it was all by my choice.

I had taken my personal freedom to choose for granted. However, the universe has a unique way of putting things into perspective when you most need it. After thirty years of continuous employment, I found myself unemployed due to corporate downsizing. I found it highly ironic, as I had been writing about how people should deal with their chance to reboot as a result of the recession. Suddenly, I found myself in the same position. I found myself needing to take my own advice. It was time to execute a well-laid-out plan and follow exactly what I was preaching. So I went about it with an outrageously positive attitude. What an opportunity it was that laid in front of me. It was what I had ordered up from the universe. I had been broadcasting to the universe that

I was done with my current job of seven years. I wanted the opportunity to make a change. Along with the change, I requested a good sum of money. There I went again, projecting statements to the universe and not being specific. When it comes to the universe, you need to be highly specific; otherwise, it will return something just as broad as your request. I asked for it, and the universe served up my walking papers and a severance package. The choice again was mine. The chance to reboot was staring me in the face. Chris, it's your kitchen, your choice.

So the question was, "What do I want to be when I grow up?" Interesting, because if you had asked me the same question twenty years ago, you would have gotten a totally different answer. What I want today is not what I wanted when I was twenty. What do you want to be? How different are you now than you were then? When I was twenty, it was all about proving myself to the world. I set very specific goals for myself, and timetables to reach those goals. I was relentless in my pursuit. It was all about getting to the next level, and although I enjoyed the process, I was never one to sit back and revel in my accomplishments. It was always on to the next level. Have you ever heard the expression "Life is wasted on the young"? I personally had problems with this phrase until I hit my forties. Suddenly a lightbulb went off in my head and things became clear. Life shifted from multiple goals to one: savor every moment. Seems like a simple idea, but in reality a tough goal to accomplish. Why? Because along with savoring every moment, the second chapter of my life seemed to have a higher purpose. The second chapter needed to be about giving more than taking. The only thing that was standing in my way was "The Machine." Yes, the machine. Although I had streamlined, it still needed to be fed. There were kids still in college and tuition needing to be paid. So how do I accomplish both? That was the question. How do I maintain The Machine while still heading in a different direction in chapter two?

I had spent the last almost thirty years of my professional career by building successful teams and coaching people. Given that fact, it would be an obvious choice to do exactly that. My body wanted to stay with the familiar; however, my heart and head wanted to go in a different direction. I had always given back to individuals; however, something was telling me that I needed to do it on a larger scale. It was time to coach and motivate worldwide. All the forces were pointing in that direction. I threw out the question to my social network, and the responses were overwhelming. Everyone was encouraging me to follow my true passion. Everyone was encouraging me to spread the sprinkles. It was time to finish the book that I had started nearly two years ago and step through the front door of chapter two. One of my favorite responses was, "Chris, you make life better!" Why not make life better, but for many more people? One of William Shakespeare's famous quotes goes as follows: *"To be or not to be, that is the question."* For me the question was not about what not to be, as my morals and foundation were firmly in place. The question was more about whether I would pursue what I believe I was truly placed on the planet to do—spread the sprinkles! In the end, it was my kitchen, my choice.

Mott-Ohs

Sometimes to make things anew involves a complete remodel. Sometimes it's necessary to rip things down to the studs and start from scratch.

Start to disturb the foundation, mess with the nucleus, or shake the center for nutrition and harmony, and it's sure to jostle any relationship mojo.

Our morals stand tall, lighting the way as a lighthouse does, guiding a wayward ship through the foggiest of nights.

It's your kitchen, your choice.

Once the aha happens, you then decide to adopt these principles, and then they become words or principles to live by—Mott-Ohs!

"To be or not to be, that is the question."

CHAPTER 5

WHO SAYS YOU CAN'T BAKE?

Have you ever heard someone say, "I can't cook," "I can't fix cars," "I can't run that far," or, moving with the theme I'm using for the book, "I can't bake"? What are they really saying? Is it that they are incapable of performing the act? Is it just that they haven't made the choice? Have they surrendered to that little voice, the voice of doubt, that may have grown from a series of negative events? Has that voice convinced them that they're incapable of doing something they really wish they could do?

Have you ever given into the doubters of the world? Those people who constantly say to you that you can't do it or shouldn't? Peer pressure often can be a huge influence, especially for those that tend to always swim with the current. *Deciding to swim against the current often takes great conviction.* The ability to block out the naysayer and steam forward is a necessary skill if you desire to be successful on your own terms. Haven't you ever caught yourself thinking or saying, "I wish I had followed my instinct rather than waiting and allowing someone else to gain all the praise, glory, or even financial rewards"? Maybe you had that special idea. Was it too much trouble to push across the finish line? Did you decide to hold off only to find out that someone got megarich off the idea? What was the difference between you and them? The difference was conviction. The only difference between the rich and famous and those that sit on the sidelines is an unwavering commitment to one's conviction.

I truly believe that there are people that were born to do certain things. Some were born to be pilots, artists, teachers, or championship athletes. When you analyze the mind-set of the truly successful, you often find that the word "can't" is not part of their vocabulary. They have this firm and overriding belief that they can and they will accomplish what they set out to do. Therefore, the possibility of failure is simply not an option.

If you had told me a year ago that I would run marathons, I would have told you that you should see a shrink. However, as of today, I have run no fewer than twenty half marathons in training. I have successfully finished one full marathon and am about to embark on the second, the Big Sur International Marathon. Yes, 26.2 of the most beautiful miles that you will find in California, but it's not without killer hills. Now for most of you, if you are honest, you can hear the voice in your head right at this moment. The voice isn't whispering, it's yelling at you. "I could never do that!" That voice is still in my head as well. The voice is saying, "Chris, you're crazy!" Today, however, there's a major difference. The difference is that a year ago, I was listening to Dr. Doubt on my right shoulder rather than listening to Mr. Sprinkles on my left. Dr. Doubt was saying, "No way, you can't do that." Mr. Sprinkles was saying, "You can do anything that you put your mind to!" So the true difference is that I have simply decided to put Dr. Doubt in his place, a safe place where he's no longer the dominant voice in my head. Take notice of the fact that he is no longer the dominant voice. Why? Because it's healthy to have some voice of caution. It's always good to examine all sides of each equation. However, *if Dr. Doubt rules your thought process, you are sure to be going nowhere fast.* He ends up eroding your self-confidence and does nothing but bring you down.

This voice is commonly referred to as the devil on your shoulder. It's the voice of negativity. It's the voice that encourages you to do things that aren't in your best interest. Many times this voice spits in the face of your moral compass. It's the voice that feeds off discouragement and allows you to be complacent. It's imperative that you stay the course. It's essential that you take the high road. I was listening to a football coach speak the other day, and he was telling a story. In the story, he explained that the devil had decided to pull up stakes and move his store from one location to another. To make the move easier, he decided to sell everything. So he advertised that he was going out of business and that everything was for sale. When he did, an innocent bystander wandered into his shop. He looked around for a while and then asked the devil to identify his best-selling item. The devil quickly replied. "Without a doubt, it's discouragement." The bystander then asked why, and the devil gladly replied, "Discouragement opens the door to that little voice on your shoulder." Discouragement is the main ingredient that craters all the rest. Once an individual starts to become discouraged, everything else falls down around him or her. If your intent is to literally go out of business, then discouragement is the best place to start.

Have you ever heard that voice? C'mon, admit it, the voice that wants to squash any attempt to deviate from the norm. Now let's face it, it's not very popular to admit that you hear voices these days. However, in this instance, you need to be real with yourself. You need to admit that Dr. Doubt or that little devil is there and that it's essential to take control. I personally am tuned in to the voices that attempt to hold me back but choose to concentrate on the ones that push me to soar to new heights. *Every morning, when I wake up, I rise to a choir of voices and a standing ovation!* It seems the older I get, the harder it is to get going, so that positive chorus of motivational voices is essential to getting out the door on the right foot.

Imagine changing just one thing. Imagine changing that voice in the morning that says, "I don't want to get up," "Do I have to go to work or school?" or "I wish it was Saturday." Instead of these negative voices, you choose to replace them with a standing ovation. A chorus of positive, reinforcing voices that sing to you, "I can't wait to get up." "I am going to accomplish so much today." "Today is going to be a great day!"

Go ahead and read the words again. This time pay attention to the feelings that are generated within your body. Take notice of your body position. As you read the negative phrases from above, your body starts to feel lethargic, lacking in energy, and you start to assume a slumping position. It's literally as if these phrases are sucking the life force right out of you. Imagine that little devil or Dr. Doubt standing on your shoulder with a huge vacuum, just waiting to suck the life energy out of you.

On the other hand, if you read the positive phrases again, you will start to feel energy building. Your body positioning will return to a position of strength and readiness. You will feel reenergized and ready to tackle anything that life can dish out. Just as the devil was sucking energy out, it's that easy to flip the switch. Sprinkles can be pumped into your body like pumping high-octane fuel into a precision race car.

Your body is merely a pawn in the game of life. The chess master is your brain. Your heart controls the board. Think about it. Often we think that our brain is making all the decisions. The reality is that our heart controls our mind. Your heart supplies blood and oxygen to the brain. Without those two elements, the brain will simply die. Without the heart, the brain makes awful choices. Much like the brain, the body has no other choice but to do exactly what the brain tells it to do. Take, for instance, the sub-four-minute mile. For decades, this superhuman goal couldn't be achieved in the sport of professional distance running. The thought was that it could never be broken. Notice I used the words "thought" and "never." This is crucially important, as *thoughts turn into perceptions and our perceptions become our reality.*

In the case of the sub-four-minute mile, a man by the name of Roger Bannister, broke the never-to-be-broken mark back on May 6, 1954. Roger was one of the few that didn't listen to the doubters. As I like to put it, he boldly jumped off the banister to achieve the unachievable. Even more amazing was that just forty-six days after breaking the record and becoming the first man to run a sub-four-minute mile, his record was broken again. Why is this? Because the mental barrier had been broken. There was no longer the perception that it couldn't be done. Rather, there was the reality that it could.

Choose to replace the voice of doubt with a positive chorus, and you will find yourself springing out of bed with a vigor rather than dragging your ass to the shower and yelling for a cup of coffee. Success is defined differently for many people. It's not always about money. It's not always about power. However, it is about the power of the positive. We have to surround ourselves with those that support us, those that believe as we do, those that are committed to baking up the perfect batch.

Mott-Ohs

Deciding to swim against the current often takes great conviction.

If Dr. Doubt rules your thought process, you are sure to be going nowhere fast.

Every morning, when I wake up, I rise to a choir of voices and a standing ovation!

Your body is merely a pawn in the game of life. The chess master is your brain. Your heart controls the board.

Our thoughts turn into perceptions and our perceptions become our reality.

CHAPTER 6

WHO'S HELPING IN THE KITCHEN?

W hether we like it or not, we are a product of our parents. Unless we realize this, we are doomed or blessed to carry on the good, the bad, and the ugly habits they have displayed throughout their lifetime. *The key to the future lies in the footsteps of the past.* Good or bad, if we learn from those footsteps, we can surely change the course of the future. We are creatures that learn by example. We see and we do. When a bird learns how to fly, it models its behavior after its parents. When a lion cub learns to hunt, it models its behavior after its parents. When a child learns to walk, it models its behavior after its parents.

My mother was one of the kindest people that I know. She spent almost fifty years in the nursing industry taking care of others. She had a selfless pursuit in life and was very happy to give more than she received. In life, I have been known to be more of a giver than a taker. Why? Because I was given a model to follow that made sense. *Give simply to give.*

At my mother's memorial, a good friend got up and spoke. She told of a time when my mother was training her to become the head of nursing at a small hospital in the Gold Country of California. As this woman spoke to a crowd of many, she explained that it was one of most stressful times in her life. She was training to be my mother's replacement. Despite the daunting task, she was calmed because she sensed that my mother would be a good teacher. She was confident that my mom would prepare her to take on the challenge of her new position. She had two weeks to learn as much as she could. She had big shoes to fill.

She explained that as the training process blew by, she became more nervous about taking on the position. Why? Because, unlike other people that explain things from step A to B, my mother was much more sophisticated. My mother knew that she couldn't hand over a manual with all the answers or describe every conceivable situation that may arise. This was not a "step A to B" job. She had to be ready to handle any step in any order. My mother knew that the best lesson would be taught through modeled behavior. Not by telling her how to do her job, but rather by showing her how.

My mother's replacement didn't realize what my mother was doing at first. It wasn't until much later that she realized that she had learned some invaluable lessons. Very skilled managers reach productivity levels not by cracking the whip, but rather by motivating people through good modeling. Often the best of managers are merely the neck that turns the head. You see, *the measure of a good manager or mentor is not merely the measure of his or her productivity, but rather* how *he or she reached that level of productivity.* The art of true management lies here. It's very easy to instruct someone to do something. It takes great skill and patience to teach solid decision-making skills.

As the two weeks drew to an end, this trainee felt like my mother really hadn't shown her anything besides the helium in her closet and the balloons and ribbon in her bottom left-hand drawer. She had helium in the closet and balloons in her bottom left-hand drawer? Yes, balloons, ribbons, and helium. As she paused and said these words to a crowd of hundreds, there was soon not a dry eye in the crowd. Yes, there was much sorrow over my mother's passing, but balloons and ribbons brought a smile to everyone's face. They knew that this was the essence of my mother. *"Phyllis had taught me the most valuable lesson of all. No matter what happens during a day, you must remain centered. You must remember where the balloons and ribbon are and celebrate the people around you. If you do, they will celebrate you in return and everything will end up okay in the end."* To this day, I have not forgotten this lesson. In this aspect, every step that I take into the future is modeled after the steps that my mother took in the past. I suppose if you were to take one lesson away from this book, this would be the one that I would pick for all of you. Love you, Mom!

My mom had taught me through modeled behavior one of the most important of life's lessons. My father, on the other hand, modeled one of the most self-destructive and detrimental. Before I explain, I must clarify. My father is a great man in his own right. He has some of the best qualities, just as my mother did. Nobody is perfect, and just as my mother had her strengths, she also had her weaknesses. From my father, I got my sense of humor, which I find to be one of my more engaging qualities. I also like to think that my father taught me to be the salesperson that I am today. However, for the sake of this example, I sacrifice my father so you may learn from our mistakes.

If you were to ask anyone who was the more flashy of the two between my mother and father, they would tell you, hands down, my dad. My dad always liked to be center stage. In keeping with this philosophy, he seemed to always be in a race with the neighbor next door. My father loved his toys, and for some reason it never seemed to be enough. My father would set his sights on something, and that something would consume him. Nothing would stop him from getting it. Once achieved, he would bask in the glory of attaining the item and then move on to the next. In one aspect, this was teaching a valuable lesson on how to pursue something you want in life with passion. However, the methods that he taught were detrimental. You see, like many Americans, my father was what I like to call an instant gratification guy—one who does whatever it takes to obtain his desire even if it's short lived and causes long-term pain or discomfort.

What exactly am I talking about? It's the dreaded credit card trap. My father was the king of credit cards. Buy now and figure out how to pay later. Through modeled behavior, I learned that if you wanted anything in life, all you needed to do was to whip out the wallet and throw down the plastic. My father used to brag about how many gold cards he had and what his credit limit was. Was he meaning to teach me such a bad lesson? I think not! But through modeled behavior, it happened. While he should have been bragging about how few credit cards he had, how low his outstanding debt was, and how many assets he had that were making money rather than costing him, he was, in turn, teaching me the opposite. Just like many of you reading this book, I too have fallen into the credit card trap in a "past life." I'm a firm believer that *sometimes in life we learn the best lessons by stepping directly into the pile of dog poop.* Sometimes in life, we need to step into it just to see how much it stinks and how hard it is to remove from our shoes.

Coupled with these bad spending habits, he also didn't like to work for a living. He made that very clear. Now don't get me wrong, my father was very successful in business. He was very good at what he did for a living. However, in the end, his financial balance sheet was askew because he wasn't smart with his money. Most of his money he squandered away through bad decisions. His pursuit and desire ended up costing him more than he could afford to give.

Am I saying to you that you shouldn't have all the comforts that life has to offer? Absolutely not! However, I am suggesting that you evaluate the real cost of obtaining those items. There should be a balance between the items you buy and the money you save for a rainy day. Just as we strive to find balance in all other areas of our lives, we must achieve balance in the area of finances. Believe me, I speak from experience. At the height of what I call my consumption era, I had thirteen televisions in my house. There were eight in the garage bar and five in other areas of the house. My cable bill was more than most people spend on groceries in a week's time. Who needs thirteen televisions in their house? I did, or at least I thought I did.

I, Chris Mott, through modeled behavior and no independent mind of my own, became a crediholic. A crediholic is an individual that is addicted to leveraging the credit card industry to obtain what he or she wants. After all, it's what everyone else is doing, right? Consume now and pay later. We are all about instant gratification in America, and I fell hook, line, and sinker into that trap. I literally went from graduating from college and having no debt to having debt large enough to sink a ship. Think about it. The house, the motorcycle, all the maintenance that accompanies them, the lifestyle, wine clubs, liquor store bills, and a combined credit card debt that was designed around making the minimum payment. My entire lifestyle was designed around consumption rather than production. Yes, I produced, but I rarely produced more than I consumed, and in most cases I consumed more than I produced. I was living on borrowed money, and my financial life was soon to be on borrowed time. Time was running out on my lifestyle. Something had to give.

Do you make the same amount of money today as you did when you first came out of college? Most likely the answer is no. Now ask yourself, "Do I have more disposable income than I did when I came out of college?" The answer again is probably no. How could this be? If I am making more money now, how could I possibly not have more disposable income? The answer lies in our consumption rates. Have you ever heard the term "graduating into your income"? It's so often true. Most of us, as we make more money, just take on more financial responsibility. With every raise there is a new acquisition. Oftentimes the acquisition is larger than the raise, and we assume the monthly payments to graduate into the more lavish lifestyle.

In my case, I was the epitome of this. My financial responsibilities became that four-hundred-pound gorilla on my back. The "in thing" these days is trying to reduce the size of your personal footprint for the good of many. In my case, there was no way to reduce my personal footprint with a four-hundred-pound gorilla on my back. I was sinking in the mud deeper and deeper with every step. I felt like I was up to my neck in quicksand and could barely breath. Again, all due to modeled behavior and no independent thoughts. Many of you are thinking that this is very similar to your own life right now. After all, the average household in America carries approximately sixteen thousand dollars of credit card debt at an average interest rate of 14 percent. Americans are leveraging themselves in the wrong direction. Instead of spending money on items that might increase their net worth, they are struggling to make the minimum monthly payment to live in the present. Every day this continues, it compromises the security of the future.

To cast away my four-hundred-pound gorilla, I needed to model my behavior after different people. I needed to do some much-needed independent thinking. I needed to evaluate who I had baking in my kitchen with me. I needed to take a good look at my consumption levels versus my production levels and truly evaluate what was making me happy in life. When I did this, I came to some shocking observations. Why did I have thirteen televisions in my house or a monthly bar bill that could stretch down the street? Was it because I dreamed and aspired to be the ultimate consumer in life? I think not. Was it because I was trying to keep up with the Joneses or trying to beat the Joneses as a result of modeled behavior? I say yes. I didn't know it at the time, but now that I am looking back, I was trying to be that guy. What kind of guy is "that guy"? It's the guy that everyone wants to be around. I had come out of an extreme ego hit. My wife had said, "I don't want you anymore." For those of you who have been divorced, and especially those of you who were on the losing end, you can relate to how hard this is. You end up questioning your self-worth in many ways. When your life is designed around another person and a family unit, it's hard to recover when that's stripped away. So what did I do? I replaced it with having just a ton of people around me. Without knowing it, I was saying to the world, "She may not want me, but all these people do." I was almost trying to buy back a sense of popularity or my self-worth. I was after it and trying to get it any way that I could. Normally when the pursuit is that intense and the definition of success is so widespread, you end up attracting all kinds of people into the mix. Not all of those people were there for the right reasons, and not all those people were helping me to get out of the rut. Most of them were just enjoying the ride. The ride was fun, but fun sometimes comes with a cost. For me, it was credit card debt that was a mile high. Putting that aside, the real cost was quality time that I lost with my children.

Let's face it. We all like to think that we surround ourselves with great people. For the most part we do. However, *everyone is not everything to everyone.* As I stated before, my father is a great man and he has a brilliant sense of humor, but when it comes to money, he is more of an expert at spending it than he is at making it. This is why I ask you, who do you have helping you in the kitchen? More importantly, what is their expertise, and are you using them in the right capacity?

As I start to evaluate the people with whom I surround myself, I often think of the game of golf. Golf is a journey. You may choose to walk or you may choose to ride. The holes on the golf course are much like the different chapters in life. Sometimes you have a good hole and sometimes you have a bad one, but you can easily erase poor performance by posting some excellent scores on the holes to come. Regardless of your skill level, each of us has a bag that we carry. In that bag, there are normally fourteen clubs, give or take. These fourteen clubs all have their specific purposes. Their general purpose is to assist us in navigating the varying terrains to accomplish the prize. Their specific purpose is to handle very select conditions. Take, for instance, the driver. The driver is made specifically to hit the ball a long distance. Very rarely would you ever pull your driver out if you needed to make a putt. Then there are the wedges. The wedges are designed for quirky shots and sometimes very difficult conditions, such as landing in tall rough or a bunker. If you were to pull your putter out to assist you in getting out of a difficult bunker, chances are you wouldn't go very far. The irons are for precision golf. Each iron is designed to hit the ball a specified distance. Judge the distance correctly, pull the appropriate iron, execute the shot, and success is yours. Then, finally, there's the putter. I liken the putter to the closer in life. You've done all the hard work to eventually reach the green, and now it's time for finesse play to sink a very small ball into a very small hole. Very rarely would you bring out a wedge, driver, or an iron to putt the ball. That would most assuredly cause you to miss your target. So again, my question to you is, why would you choose to pull the wrong club to assist you in a clutch situation? The object in golf, as in life, is to ensure that you have the right tools in your bag. Once you obtain the right tools, it's a matter of choosing the right one to assist you at the right time.

I was asked the other day how my balance sheet looked. The individual who was asking me was specifically talking about my financial status and how my assets stacked up against my liabilities. When calculating a balance sheet, you are considered to be in better financial shape if your assets outweigh your liabilities. The question got me thinking. Rather than focusing only on our financial balance sheets, we should be evaluating our balance sheet for life. Much of what we are talking about in this book is becoming balanced in all areas. Just as a financial balance sheet weighs your financial assets against your financial liabilities, we must identify those people in our lives that are either assets or liabilities. I like to think of this exercise as assessing your "person-al balance sheet."

To have a well-balanced "person-al balance sheet," it's essential for you to surround yourself with a good mix of individuals in your kitchen. One individual may be your spiritual advisor, while the next might be your financial advisor. One person might be your lover, and the next is a confidant. Once you realize the importance of individuals, it will be easier for you to gain balance and, even more so, the competitive edge that you require in life. *Calling on people to assist you in life is much like pulling the right club out of the bag in the game of golf.*

It's essential that you become adept at identifying those that support you in whatever course you choose to take in life. It's equally or even more essential that you be able to identify those that tend to slow you down or even stand in the way of accomplishing your goals. This is sometimes tricky, because those that support you the most may not be the best people to call upon for advice in some situations. Take, for instance, smoking. If you are trying to quit, smokers are probably not the best folks to surround yourself with in that instance. They would most likely support your desire to continue, rather than your need to stop.

If it's an extremely healthy lifestyle that you seek, are you surrounding yourself with extremely healthy people? If it's great wealth or financial stability, are you surrounding yourself with those successful in money management? If you examine those around you through your own lens of success, light will be shed on why you are lacking in certain areas and why you tend to excel in others. There is typically a direct correlation between the areas in which your life is lacking and the level of expertise that surrounds you.

Take time to identify the key players in your life and their respective roles in adding to your asset list. Everyone must be carefully placed or balanced to support you in specific aspects of your life. It's imperative to clarify and understand their role. We often find ourselves making the mistake of asking the wrong person for advice at the wrong time. Think about it. Would you go and solicit advice from an attorney if you were growing tomatoes? Would you ask your automotive mechanic for advice if you were feeling ill? I think not. So often, we turn to the wrong people for advice when they have no business offering it. We tend to ask our parents for financial advice when they don't have a good track record of managing their own money. We often ask our spouse for career advice when they have limited knowledge of our field of work. Have you ever heard the expression "Garbage in, garbage out"? *Once you recognize that each person has a specific role in your life, it will enrich your time with them and increase your overall balance in life.*

Take, for instance, marriage. Have you ever heard spouses say that their partner is attempting to change them? They are trying to train them to be the perfect companion. This happens, more often than not, because people want their spouse to be everything. This is where many people go wrong. Whether it's with a spouse, friend, family member, or anyone else, everyone that you choose to surround yourself with has strengths and weaknesses. It's your job as the head baker in your kitchen to recognize this. Adding people's strengths to your mixture for success is a vital step in baking the perfect batch. By recognizing their weaknesses, you can decide to cast away those ingredients that don't add to the mixture. For instance, if you're an opera lover and your husband is not, don't drag him to the opera. In the end, you both will be miserable. Find someone who enjoys the same passion. Take that person with you instead. Use it as an opportunity to form a new friendship and, while doing so, encourage your spouse to enjoy something apart from you. Guaranteed, it will be a win-win situation for all. You will reunite more refreshed and appreciative of each other. *Once you play to the strength in others, you will often find that they are your biggest cheerleaders.* They are the ones who encourage rather than discourage. It's imperative that you hand pick people that will add to your personal balance sheet. They must sing your praises on the road to personal success.

Take time to visit my Web site at www.mottivation.com. Download your free version of my "person-al balance sheet." Identify the people that surround you. Determine whether you consider them assets or liabilities. You must identify both assets and liabilities, as this will remind you when you should or shouldn't enlist their support. Remember, *we don't need to be the master of all aspects of our lives, but we do need to surround ourselves by mastery.*

Mott-Ohs

The key to the future lies in the footsteps of the past.

Give simply to give.

The measure of a good manager or mentor is not merely the measure of his or her productivity, but rather *how* he or she reached that level of productivity.

"Phyllis had taught me the most valuable lesson of all. No matter what happens during a day, you must remain centered. You must remember where the balloons and ribbon are and celebrate the people around you. If you do, they will celebrate you in return and everything will end up okay in the end."

Sometimes in life we learn the best lessons by stepping directly into the pile of dog poop.

Everyone is not everything to everyone.

Calling on people to assist you in life is much like pulling the right club out of the bag in the game of golf.

Once you recognize that each person has a specific role in your life, it will enrich your time with them and increase your overall balance in life.

Once you play to the strength in others, you will often find that they are your biggest cheerleaders.

We don't need to be the master of all aspects of our lives, but we do need to surround ourselves by mastery.

CHAPTER 7

FROM SCRATCH OR STORE BOUGHT?

W hen I hit middle school age, my parents decided to move from the West Coast to the backwoods in the East. Talk about culture shock! I was transported from sunny California, the land of OP shorts and mid-seventies temperatures, to the land of flannel and long underwear. My mid-seventies were quickly replaced with 70 percent humidity and take-your-breath-away wind chill.

East Coast excitement consisted of the Weather Channel, snow days, and cooking maple syrup. Have you ever made maple syrup? It's literally about as much fun as watching sap ooze from a tree. It would take days and days of transporting sap from the trees to a large boiling pot. It was a continuous process, boiling gallons and gallons of sap through a very smoky process down to a fine substance called syrup. I believe the conversion rate is like ten to one. You must boil down ten gallons of sap to generate one very prized gallon of syrup. Sounds great, doesn't it? At the time, I was shaking my head at the idea of the relocation. You see, for a bursting-at-the-seams teenager, it seemed at times like a death sentence. What? It takes thirty minutes to drive to the nearest town? Shoot me now! After all, in those days, there was no Internet, no video games, and the revolution of the century was the compact disc. What was a teenager to do?

To this day, I love to camp, and for this reason only: I'm able to transport my kids to an environment that is free from Web surfing, cell phones, texting, and video games to a place that is filled with late-night chats around a campfire, s'mores, hunting for crawdads in a stream, or building a sand castle on a beach. Yes, the thought of prying the cell phone or the video games from your child's hands may be a scary one; however, I promise, it will be the best move you ever make! I assure you, there will be resistance initially. However, kids know how to be kids. It's instinctual. I truly believe that God gave us imaginations before he gave us wisdom. Albert Einstein once said, *"Imagination is more important than knowledge."* I believe this to be true, as imagination can instantly transport you wherever you want to be. *Imagination is the key to unlocking the door to whatever you seek in the universe. You can't be what you can't imagine.* There are no boundaries. You can truly be what you aspire to be, and the mind has no choice but to follow. I say, give a child a cardboard box and he or she will transform it into a castle. Give children a creek and they will surf the rapids for days. Give children an oak tree and they will climb its branches as if they were monkeys.

Even if it wasn't calculated, I like to think that my parents made a conscious decision to help me appreciate the simpler things. Perhaps they had a grand plan: stop the wheel of life from flying by and allow me to savor every moment. After all, my parents were experienced veterans by the time I came along. They had raised three children. They always said they experimented on the rest, now it's time for the best! LOL. I was a mistake. However, make no mistake about it, after raising three kids in varied environments, they knew what was important and had my best interest in mind. Just like the sap that we were cooking into maple syrup, they brought me down to a slow boil. They transformed what could have been a very turbulent time into a prized jug of maple syrup.

Often in life, we don't know what's truly good for us. Many times in life, we are like ships drifting at sea without a rudder. I like to think that people or circumstances will normally guide us in the right direction. What I perceived as incarceration on the East Coast ended up being one of the best experiences in my life. My dad and mom knew exactly what they were doing. It's ironic, because I would trade anything to return to those days and watch my mother, with such vigor and conviction, boiling that sap down to maple syrup. She was so proud of herself for sticking to the process and making that prized gallon. When she was finished, my father had to literally hose her down and burn her clothes in the front yard. She smelled so bad from all the smoke!

As I fished for days with my father alone on a lake, we developed a bond that nobody could ever replace. As I transported gallons of sap to my smoky mother, a sparkle in my eye developed that no man could ever extinguish. The warmth of flannel, no matter how hideous it appeared, became comfortable, and the snow day became the prize. Have you ever made the comment on Monday, "I can't wait until it's Friday"? I'm sure you have. I think that my dad and mom were trying to instill the idea that every day was a gift. Every day should be savored and never taken for granted. After all, look at the calculations of that one simple statement: "I can't wait until it's Friday." You just blew away four days of the week. Four days times fifty-two weeks in a year, then applied to the average life expectancy of seventy years, results in 14,560 wasted days in your life. Knowing that, would you really choose to discount Monday through Thursday, or would you choose to seize every day?

My question to you is simply this: do you prefer store bought or made from scratch? I can remember when my kids were young and, for special occasions, they would make presents in school. The time and effort expended was priceless. You could literally see the sprinkles in their eyes as they waited eagerly for you to unwrap the gift. If I had to answer the same question, I would without a doubt answer, "Made from scratch." Why is it so special? It's so special because of the sweat equity put into creation. Sweat equity always puts things in proper perspective and makes the experience and the giving special.

When it comes to ourselves, it seems as if we are trying to order up our lifestyles and/or our appearance. To prove my point, we, as Americans, spent over thirteen billion dollars on cosmetic enhancing procedures in 2009. This monumental expenditure was mostly in pursuit of the quick fix or ideal look. This leads me to believe that most Americans prefer store bought. They are after instant gratification and will pay for it. Makes you wonder a bit, doesn't it? Could this possibly be better than "from scratch"?

In a previous chapter, I made the argument that when things are readily available and easily obtained, they are often taken for granted. As things are taken for granted, they lose their value. Think about that gallon of prized maple syrup. If you simply pull it off the shelf and pay five dollars for it, it's not coveted. What makes it special? However, if you spend hours and hours of effort to make or achieve it, then it's cherished or even prized. I can remember eating that homemade maple syrup. Every time that jug was pulled from the refrigerator, the room would go silent. It was like royalty had just entered the room. We knew a real treat was on its way! It was the best maple syrup ever because of the love and effort put into creating it. Everything is better if love and effort are included.

So let's drill down a bit. What exactly are you trying to achieve, accomplish, or fulfill in life? For me, one of my goals as of late was to finish a marathon. Can you imagine if I was able to walk into a store and simply buy what was needed to prepare for a marathon? "I'll take one Instant Marathon Runner Kit, please." How anticlimactic would that be? In reality, I had to spend countless miles and hours training for my first marathon. The sense of achievement that I felt when I crossed the finish line was something that I cannot describe. I had just accomplished what was once an impossibility in my mind. The medal that was placed around my neck is something that I will forever look at and say, "Wow, I did that!" I guarantee you, if I simply bought the preparation from the store, the medal would just be sitting on some shelf collecting dust right now. Easy come, easy go. So again, my vote is for "made from scratch."

You can't cheat when you are pursuing happiness in life. There are no short-cuts. You can't go into a store and buy it. You can't rent it. You can't steal it. There is only one way to get it, and it's the old-fashioned way. It has to come from scratch. Some of the most unhappy people that I know try often to buy it. They surround themselves with weak substitutes for the real deal. They skip the steps, use poor ingredients, and fail to follow through with the process. Follow the steps, use the proper ingredients, and put the effort into completing each step in the process, and I guarantee a huge batch of happiness.

Mott-Ohs

"Imagination is more important than knowledge."—Albert Einstein

Imagination is the key to unlocking the door to whatever you seek in the universe.

You can't be what you can't imagine.

CHAPTER 8

THE RECIPE IS YOUR ROAD MAP

A re you one of those people who buy something and, instead of reading the directions first, you are immediately hard at work trying to put it together without using directions? Are you one of those people who resort to the directions only after you have made multiple failed attempts? If you are, I must ask you, why? Why do you do this to yourself? We have so many tools surrounding us to assist in the direction department. If you were to drive from point A to point B, you would either grab your archaic map or, better yet, a newfangled GPS navigation system. Electronics come with installation instructions. Medication comes clearly marked with dosage and frequency instructions. The list goes on and on. So, I ask you, why would you choose to make things harder on yourself? I have news: *the secret to a happy, fruitful life is not rocket science.* Life does not have to be difficult.

Included on every box of cupcake mix is the key to success. The key is clearly marked as "baking instructions." Every step of the way is specifically spelled, measured, and timed out for you. All organized in an easy-to-follow recipe to ensure that your cupcakes are perfect every time. It's all explained from point A to point B. It's just a matter of whether you choose to use it or not. In life, you simply need to follow the directional signs provided for you. We are so good at obeying traffic signals. However, when it comes to life, we aren't as good at listening to the traffic cop in our head yelling "stop," "go," or "continue with caution."

Wouldn't it be nice if life came with baking instructions? Life would be perfect just as long as we followed the recommended steps. If only we could take the guesswork out of life and it was explained for us. Can you imagine the chapters? Raising teens would be an amazingly long chapter! It would have topics such as *Shorts That are Way Too Short, Excessive Alcohol Consumption,* and *The Parents' Guide for Maintaining Sanity While Raising Your Kids. Successful Relationships* would be worth reading. *How to Succeed in Business* would be a "must read." So would *Living Healthy and Maintaining Balance,* and the list goes on.

Life may not come with a specific set of baking instructions, but each of us has been blessed with the ultimate built-in navigation system. Your internal navigation system is known as your five senses. Yes, most of us can see, smell, taste, touch, and hear. Each one of these senses is highly in tune with the world around us. They can spot trouble on the horizon and lead us to greener pastures. It's only when we take these senses for granted or pay little attention that we get into trouble.

When our five senses work in harmony, the synergy creates a sixth sense, a keen intuition. The formal definition of the sixth sense is: a power of perception seemingly independent of the five senses. Once keen intuition kicks in, you tend to feel less and know more. All the five senses are talking to you in their own way and sending messages to your brain, which in turn translates into keen intuition. I have talked about positive and negative voices before. The voice of keen intuition is one voice that you should definitely listen to in life. It's normally looking out for your best interest.

Let's examine the traditional five senses, as they're all key players in baking up that ideal batch in life.

Hearing: Face it, we suck at listening. We need to become better listeners. Life often speaks to us, but very few of us can hear what it's saying. Is it a hearing issue or is it our willingness to listen? Perhaps, it's that *we are so consumed with our next thought that we rarely pay attention to the thought at hand.* We need to slow down and live in the moment! Life seems to have a way of showing us the way. Often the road map appears as doors opening or closing.

Many times these doors open and shut without us taking advantage of the opportunities that lie behind them. Why? Because *life speaks quietly. It's imperative that we listen intently.* The doors of opportunity swing open making little noise. It's up to you to train your ears so you may listen for them. Once you notice the doors, you will be shown the way to whatever you wish to accomplish in life. You will hold the key not only to listening, which is a great attribute, but to the art of communicating. Carl Rogers, an influential American psychologist, once said, "Man's inability to communicate is a result of his failure to listen effectively."

Any good salesperson will tell you that the secret to amazing sales performance lies in the ears and not on the tip of your tongue. When a salesperson learns to listen, he or she becomes extremely efficient in the art of communication. I can remember back to my first days as a leasing consultant in the apartment management industry. I thought I was the bomb when it came to leasing! I was armed with tons of information. I knew my product thoroughly and I had done my homework on the competition. I was busting at the seams with information and couldn't wait to tell people about it. My enthusiasm was unsurpassed, and after a couple of months, I was the epitome of what I like to call "the Disneyland tour." The Disneyland tour is best described as the following: You jump on the bus and you are literally given the tour for the next twenty to thirty minutes. No interaction is required. Yes, I thought I was the bomb. Little did I know, I was bombing out. Sure, my closing ratio was respectable; however, it wasn't until I was sent to my first seven-day sales training that I realized that I was doing it all wrong. I was taught that the art of sales is not solely about conveying what you know. It's more about listening to your prospect and then conveying information that is tailored to your prospect's needs. Once this is achieved, the prospect has little choice but to commit. After I returned from my training session, I realized that I had been using "the shotgun approach." Yes, I was firing information in a wide pattern with the hopes of something hitting my target. Little did I know that my target was tuning out and losing interest because my presentation didn't apply to his or her specific needs or desires. After I was taught that listening was my road map, it was the key to gaining people's trust and capturing their interest. I quickly realized that I could shoot like a sniper. Listening gave me pinpoint accuracy. Every piece of information that left the tip of my tongue was a direct hit. My presentation went from being "canned" and deserving nothing but the trash can to one that was highly skilled and tailored to the prospect. I had mastered the art of communication, and, little did I know, it didn't just apply to leasing apartments. The art of listening can diffuse any difficult situation. It can keep you on course in your relationships and can bring you great success in your career. *Those that have something to prove will choose to speak. Those that don't will choose to listen.*

Sight: Just as there are signs to direct us down the road, there are also directionals to navigate the twists and turns that life has to offer. Most of these signs present themselves as nonverbal communication. Nonverbal communication or body language comes as facial expressions, gestures, eye contact, posture, and even the tone of our voice. Just as it's vitally important to master the art of listening, it's also equally important for you to master the art of deciphering nonverbal communication. You see, we tend to like people who are similar to ourselves, so emulating the speech patterns, tone, and body language of the person we are communicating with puts us on the road to instant rapport. This is called matching and mirroring. If you think about it, I bet you do this automatically. Do you have loud, high energy friends? Do you notice yourself acting louder to match their tone? There you go, matching and mirroring.

If I had mastered the art of nonverbal communication earlier on in my marriage, I might still be married. Non verbal communication isn't just about relationships. It's an important skill for business as well. Every person gives off certain nonverbal signals. It's important in negotiation to know and understand the technique of matching and mirroring. By becoming a master at this technique, you become a master communicator by seeing all the signs that life throws at you.

Touch: Beyond saving you from burning or cutting yourself, the sense of touch can guide you to a life of fulfillment beyond your imagination. As a child, I would get so excited about Christmas, so much so that I could hardly sleep on Christmas Eve. I couldn't wait to get my hands on and touch the gifts that were waiting under the tree. At some point in life, these unsophisticated and selfish feelings shifted. At some point, I began to derive more joy out of giving and watching the reaction of others than vice versa. The things that truly touch me today, I had no idea existed as a child. My feelings are much more sophisticated than in my youth. Whether it's you stirring the emotions of others or your emotions being stirred, you must realize that the power of touch is an amazing idea. Touch has healing powers beyond comprehension. When we are touched personally, we are best served to pay attention. Touch is not only a valuable sense, but it comes with great responsibility. I truly believe that we were put on this planet to touch the lives of others.

Taste: How does life taste to you? You can normally tell if items are appealing or, even more so, safe to consume by their taste. Often in the baking process, we tend to take a taste here or there to determine whether we are on track or not. It's similar to dipping your toe into the pool to test the waters. Is the water too cold, too hot, or just right? Our sense of taste is not exclusive to tasting food. We often know and refer to things as "distasteful" in life. We tend to avoid those things and/or people that do not appeal to our personal palate. We also tend to refrain from partaking in distasteful activities. Taste, in a nutshell, is a very powerful sense.

Smell: Smell is an interesting sense. It can instantly stir certain emotions and transport you back in time through the process of triggering memories. It can steer you away from danger when you smell a gas leak or smoke. I have heard this, as I personally lack the ability to smell. Yes, I am handicapped in this one area of my life. I have lacked the ability to smell as long as I can remember. Can you imagine not being able to smell? Most of you would then question how one would taste. Many times when we lose one sense, the body finds a way to compensate for the handicap. In many cases our body responds with acute senses in return. In other words, our other senses climb to new levels. No, I don't have x-ray vision, supersonic hearing, or the healing touch, but I do believe that my sense of taste has rebounded in a certain way. Nonetheless, I lack the ability to smell certain things. Like anything else in life, it has its pros and cons. I lack the ability to smell my girlfriend's perfume; however, on the flip side, if she were to pass gas, I would be spared that simple pleasure as well. :-)

Intuition: Intuition is the culmination of all the above. It's the net result of all your senses working in perfect harmony. Intuition isn't acquired straight out of the gate. It's developed over time as we become more in tune with all the five senses. Intuition is one of life's biggest assets. Life does not come with a road map. It's often up to us to decipher the signs that life has to offer. By sending out our navigation experts, known as the five senses, we can thoroughly test and check out these signs from all directions. After our discovery is done, intuition kicks in and is sure to guide us in the right direction. This book is essentially your road map or baking instructions for life. However, life can be unpredictable. The baking process itself is straightforward; however, you are inevitably going to have obstacles thrown into the mix. There are going to be distractions along the way. There will be disasters in the kitchen. There will be times that your pantry is lacking the ingredients necessary. There will be times that the folks that you have chosen to assist you in the kitchen fall short of your expectations. Regardless of how much life throws at you, you must commit to yourself that you will always return to the course. If you are thrown off, you must listen to your internal navigation system that is saying, "Recalculating!" You must rely on your intuition.

We, as individuals, must be able to adapt. *Those that refuse to follow the winding path of life and demand to walk a straight line are destined to step off a cliff.* We all have stepped off a cliff or two. I personally have stepped off many. At an early age, I had life all planned out. The plan included a college degree, getting married, having kids, and living happily ever after. I guess how the last part of that sentence is written is quite telling. I got married, but I should have written "get married and stay married." Now that the dust has settled, the "happily ever after" part of the equation is happening. It was never in the grand plan to get divorced. I never had a plan B, nor do most people when they fully commit. We don't necessarily plan for detours, as we very rarely plan for anything other than success. As I look back at the situation, I probably shouldn't have been so blind to my surroundings. They say love is often blind, and in life being blind is not without its risks. Can you imagine trying to bake a batch of cupcakes blindfolded? What a mess the kitchen would be. When my detour arrived, I was ill equipped to deal with the change in direction. It took me longer to recover since I was caught off guard. Why was I caught off guard? Even though I was a good spouse and father, I was not well balanced. I had dedicated myself so much to my wife and children that it was an unhealthy state of balance.

In life, the farther you climb the ladder, the longer and harder the fall. Many people are now thinking, well, let's just not climb the ladder. That's not what I am saying at all. *If you don't climb the ladder, you will never see the incredible view from the top.* However, while you're climbing the ladder, take time to appreciate the different rungs. If you are focused only on getting to the top, you are sure to be somewhat one-dimensional when you get there. If you branch out with every step, you will be more well versed and well balanced while standing at the top. I was "that guy" that believed that to be faithful, you needed to have tunnel vision. I was "that guy" that was focused on one thing and one thing only. In the end, my one-dimensional definition of success in life sent me down a one-way street sure to hit a dead end. We need to be constantly thinking of multiple routes. We need to be extremely flexible when it comes to following life's recipe for success.

On many occasions we need to be prepared to write our own directions. We have to define our own road map to success. This often can work in our favor. Take, for example, salespeople who cold call prospective clients for a living. Cold calling, the practice of calling prospective clients out of the blue, has always been revered as one of the most difficult sales skills to master. Why? Because most people perceive it as a win/lose proposition. Your results from cold calling are either productive or not. Most people are afraid of rejection, so the idea of receiving an immediate yes or no is enough for some to say, "No way, that profession is not for me." However, truly successful salespeople will tell you that they have redefined the rules of cold calling. They have taken a win/lose proposition and written their own directions. They have essentially taken their baking instructions and rewritten them to make the process not only more palatable but more successful and rewarding. They set themselves up for success by redefining the goals of the call. The number one goal is to simply make contact. This primary goal is achieved 100 percent of the time through persistence. The secondary goal is to have an excuse by the end of the call to follow up. This is an easy goal to accomplish. Last, but not least, is to ask if they are in need of your services. If they are not, you then ask for a referral of someone that may be looking to hire someone with your expertise. By redefining the objectives of the call in this manner, the cold call just went from a scary proposition of rejection to a win/win situation every time. This is just one specific example, but you can literally write your own recipe for success for any given situation. Get writing! Develop your recipe. Listen to your internal navigation system and your keen intuition. Map out your road map to success!

Mott-Ohs

The secret to a happy, fruitful life is not rocket science.

We are so consumed with our next thought that we rarely pay attention to the thought at hand.

Life speaks quietly. It's imperative that we listen intently.

Any good salesperson will tell you that the secret to amazing sales performance lies in the ears and not on the tip of your tongue.

Those that have something to prove will choose to speak. those that don't will choose to listen.

Those that refuse to follow the winding path of life and demand to walk a straight line are destined to step off a cliff.

If you don't climb the ladder, you will never see the incredible view from the top.

CHAPTER 9

SOMETIMES THE PROCESS ISN'T PRETTY

My brother is a painter. I'm not. My brother paints with great care. I, on the other hand, look like a live abstract painting by the time I'm finished. Although our form and methods are different, in the end, we have both accomplished our goal. Sometimes it's not about how you get from point A to point B but rather that you just get to point B.

I've talked a lot about my experiences as a runner because many of the thoughts in this book originated out on the asphalt. Before the thoughts could flow, there were miles and miles of struggle. Once I pushed past the pain, the ideas would flow and develop. As I got stronger, they seemed to strengthen into chapters. As I talk about the ingredients and perseverance for happiness, I would be remiss not to talk about the process, as they go hand in hand.

Have you ever heard anyone refer to an "ugly win"? Maybe you have heard someone say, "I got it done, but it wasn't pretty." They were referring to the process. Take, for instance, championship figure skating. Do you think these athletes step out onto the ice and knock out triple axels or the intimidating quad without hours of work? I don't think so. You only see them on the day of the competition after years and countless hours of practice. This process often involves falls and, in many cases, injuries along the way.

Recently, I ran the Big Sur Marathon. For those of you unfamiliar with this part of California, this is some of the most majestic scenery found in the United States. Highway 1 travels from Big Sur northward. As you leave the towering redwoods that surround the little town of Big Sur, you travel along coastal cliffs. You come across winding roads with stellar views of cliffside beaches and kelp-filled oceans. This scenery continues for 26.2 miles, all until you hit the town of Carmel. This stretch of highway is the official route of the Big Sur Marathon. As you can imagine, it's not without its fair share of hills. The most notorious is Hurripain Point, a grueling two-mile incline. With Tongan drummers at the bottom, we attacked the climb with vigor and arrived at the top victorious to cheering crowds and a concert pianist. But, after a brief pause for pictures, reality set in. There were 14.2 miles yet to finish.

We continued to crank along the coastal highway, mile after mile, and at mile eighteen, it started to hit me. I had been having some knee problems in training and my right knee especially would start to ache and weaken after mile fifteen. Go figure, right? Well, I had made it eighteen miles and it started to kick in. I continued to struggle for the next two miles, and it came to a point where I needed to walk. My best friend, Craig, was running with me, and despite his encouragement, my body was getting the best of me. I can remember his words. He was literally using my own words against me. He said, "There may be a day, but this is not the day!" These were the words I had used on him as he embarked on his training. I had told Craig that running was 25 percent physical ability and 75 percent mental fortitude. Running is a very lonely sport, and it's just you and your body out on the road for hours at a time. Once you push past the pain, there is much time to think. It almost becomes a state of meditation. However, when you stretch into the later miles of your run, the meditation is interrupted again by your body talking. This is when mental fortitude comes into play. I explained to Craig that there would be times that his body would scream at him and that it would come up with every reason in the world to stop. It would be up to him to push back the pain and to purposely push those interrupting voices aside. I was a true believer in the advice. However, until the Big Sur Marathon, I had never hit what many call "the wall." I came close in the San Francisco Marathon, but until mile twenty of Big Sur, I had never experienced what I call "total system failure." Yes, my body had reached its breaking point, and despite my efforts to fight away the voices, I had to bring it down a notch. I was forced by my body to walk.

This part of the process wasn't pretty. I had so much confidence in my mental fortitude that I truly believed that this would never happen. In the long run, my mental fortitude was overtaken by my physical limitations. When I finally could do nothing more than give in to that voice and walk, my posture became that of a defeated man. My head that had been held high for the previous twenty miles began to hang. My breath, although I was no longer running, was still panting with every step. I was defeated, and you could see it with every step that I took. There were 6.2 miles left and I had time to listen to my body with every step. I was disgusted at myself for walking and had plenty of time to think about it. At the average walking pace of fifteen minutes per mile, I had an hour and a half ahead to listen to *that* voice.

Bottom line, I finished the marathon and got my medal. I never intended to walk, but as a result, I learned a lot about myself that day. The walk was a bigger struggle due to my physical and mental anguish. With every person that passed me, both young and old, male and female, it took more out of me to dive into the well of mental fortitude to make it through. Despite the majestic scenery along the way, this was definitely an ugly win. The experience was not pretty at all. However, after I finished, I looked back on the race and told myself that no matter what the circumstance, I would never lower my head again. I can remember passing the event photographers. Each time that I did, I would lower my head, as I didn't want them to see my face.

I then looked at the pictures afterwards and realized that it was the wrong thing to do. I should have been proud that I had made it that far. I should have been proud that after a year of setting a goal, I was about to finish one of the hardest marathons in existence. I learned that day what Ernest Hemingway said best: "courage is grace under pressure."

I didn't set out to walk that day, nor did I set out to learn some of life's most important lessons. However, that's often the way of the world. Some of the best things in life are stumbled upon. Mistakes are often the birthplace of innovation. If you don't believe me, just research Velcro, Silly Putty, Wheaties, and penicillin, to name just a few. These are just some examples in an infinite list of success stories that started as mishaps. Just like the baking process, life can get messy at times. It's up to us to pay little attention to the mess along the way. It's up to us to hold steady in our conviction. Whether you're a parent, supervisor, student, new business owner, or public figure, it's your responsibility to lead by example, especially when things are burning in the kitchen. *Anyone can be a role model when life is a cupcake. The true leaders and people of character step up and hold their head up high when the kitchen is burning down around them.*

Mott-Ohs

Anyone can be a role model when life is a cupcake. The true leaders and people of character step up and hold their head up high when the kitchen is burning down around them.

CHAPTER 10

WHAT'S IN THE PANTRY?

Have you ever heard the expression "Never judge a book by its cover"? We all do it. In fact, many of us pride ourselves on being able to size a person up in seconds. For those of you that do, if you're being honest, you would admit that your initial assessment is not totally accurate most of the time. Why is this? Because *the door to the pantry can look very different than what's contained inside.* In other words, even though first impressions are important, the book's cover is not always a good indication of the content within. The front door is not always an accurate indication of the overall condition of one's pantry.

Nonetheless, so many people do make quick judgments, so first impressions are crucial. In fact, in sales and when biding for a new job, professional coaches will teach you that you will never get a second chance to make a first impression. Why is this so important? It's important because we all know that the first impression sticks with people and takes much to overcome. If the first impression is blown, it often takes ten positive encounters to counteract the negative impression. Many times, you don't even get the chance to counteract or recover. You must *put your best foot forward at all times, no matter what the circumstance.*

I was talking to one of my dearest friends the other day. He has been unemployed for some time and was asking my advice to revamp and freshen up his cover letter and resume. I asked about the current length of his cover letter. His reply was, "two paragraphs." Now listen up, folks. This advice is born from years and years of reviewing resumes. The most important part of a cover letter is the first three sentences. Why? Because cover letters and resumes are like billboards; the reader is most likely flying by them at sixty-five to seventy-five miles per hour. You literally have maybe five to ten seconds to catch their attention, make a lasting first impression, and leave them wanting more. You want them to open the door to the pantry.

Think about how successful billboards would be if they had two paragraphs of information on them. They would have zero impact on their intended audience because the message would be lost in a blur. *Often in life, too much information is a bad thing.* This is a hard lesson to learn. It's hardest to learn in your youth. I can remember sitting in meetings fresh out of college. I was literally busting at the seams with enthusiasm. My motto at the time was, "They are paying me for my two cents, so I am going to give them their money's worth and then some." There was this overwhelming urge to prove my worth to those around me and those that hired me. Little did I know, they were paying me to speak but more so to listen and learn. Consider this. If you are constantly concentrating on what you're going to bust out with next, how can you truly be listening? Those that master the art of listening often absorb the message and actually move down the road of life at a much faster pace than those who don't. If you are paying attention, your input will be well received. An active listener listens with a purpose. The purpose is to learn and find clues. Once the active listener discovers these clues, he zeroes in on his target and takes it down with precision. He leaves little of his potential success to luck.

Being selective with your words is truly one of the most valuable talents that you can acquire. It's a two-pronged talent that consists of two factors: one, being selective about the words that you let cross your lips, and two, being selective about the timing of sharing those words. There is a time to talk and others that are made for shutting up. Often you will find that great respect is gained by being strategic regarding when and where you decide to give your two cents. You will find that people will step into trouble right in front of you due to opening their mouth at an inopportune moment. *What you say is just as important as when you say it.*

Billboards have catchy phrases and stunning images that catch your eye. They are designed to catch your attention and leave a lasting impression. Resumes have traditionally been anything but that. In fact, the resume, although it has been tweaked here and there, has virtually remained unchanged throughout the years. I can remember sitting in a business-writing course in college and being taught the proper format for a resume. As I review resumes even today, I'm amazed that they all come in the same vanilla format. Hello! What is the entire point of a resume? A resume should serve as your personal billboard; one which catches the eye of a prospective employer and leaves a lasting impression. Ultimately, it should motivate your audience to want more and make a call. Being vanilla (bland) does nothing towards accomplishing that goal. In fact, it's sure to land you in a stack of soon-to-be-forgotten resumes.

Why hasn't the resume changed over the years? As I was discussing the cover letter with my out-of-work friend, it came to me. It hasn't changed because the people that are writing them haven't changed. This fact supports the entire premise of the book. America is stuck in a vanilla rut. We, as Americans, have lost our sprinkles. We are lacking the sprinkles that set us apart from all the rest. We are lacking the sprinkles that attract attention and leave a lasting impression. It's time to find our sprinkles again and start broadcasting them to the world immediately.

Seriously, if I were to write my resume today, I would change everything. It wouldn't be on conventional sized paper. It wouldn't be delivered in an envelope. In those first three sentences, there would be a link to my virtual resume on line. Nothing about my resume would be conventional. Contemplate this. If you only have one chance to make a first impression, what does a white envelope or a standard e-mail say about you? What does it accomplish to set you apart from the field? I say, nothing! In fact, I wouldn't even call it a resume. Let's be creative and brainstorm together. What catchy phrase exists that conveys that this personal billboard is far from the norm? How do we pique someone's interest from the get-go? This is not merely a resume, but rather a reflection of who you are as an individual, professional, or asset to their team. It's a statement of what you have learned over the years and/or your accomplishments. It's your body of work! If you would like to see my most recent resume, take a look at www.mottivation.com. It's sure to impress you!

As approximately sixteen million unemployed Americans sit in the vanilla rut, their self-confidence erodes by the day. With every day that passes without the offer of employment, they are constantly reminded as the sun rises and sets that they are unwanted. They are continually challenged to maintain their level of self-confidence, and even though they try, they find themselves continually comparing themselves to those that are employed. After all, when you're lacking confidence, it's extremely hard to continually sell yourself on the positive, because the negative is standing right in front of you. *Time can either be your friend or foe* when it comes to being unemployed or in a transitional state in your life.

If your pantry looks good from the outside but is lacking on the inside, you must take advantage of the time. Again, it's your choice. It's your choice to either make the most of your time or wallow in your self-pity. You can choose to either reinvest in yourself or become one with the couch. It's one thing to have a great billboard, but when it comes time to put up or shut up, you must produce. With so many out of work, the job of getting a job has become extremely competitive. Whether you are a recent graduate or a seasoned veteran, you must ask yourself the honest questions: How does my pantry stack up against the rest? Does it house all the proper ingredients? Is it equipped to bake the perfect batch of cupcakes? Is it well organized and feeding my recipe for success? If all the ingredients are there, sprinkles will never be the issue. Bake me the perfect cupcake and there will always be plenty of sprinkles to go around!

Take a moment to really assess whether your pantry is in order and stocked. What are your priorities at this point? It's time to discover your true passion. How are you going to pursue those passions? Take a moment to determine where you really want to be and where you're going? You must determine what type of ingredients you need to accomplish each goal. Determine if certain areas of your pantry are depleted in any way shape or form. If this is indeed the case, it's time to reinvest in your pantry.

Allow me to put this into a relatable experience. Before meeting my current girlfriend, I was actively involved in the cyberdating scene. When I eventually decided to dive in, I realized that we, as Americans, cocoon. "Cocooning" is the process of becoming more self-contained by the minute and venturing out less. By doing so, we diminish our opportunities when it comes to fate happening. The by-chance meeting of the past has gone by the wayside. We need to get out there and make it happen, no matter what we are looking to achieve in life. I'm a true salesman at heart and know that the more bushes that I rustle, the more opportunities will fly out. As a result of this dating endeavor, I have finetuned my approach when it comes to sizing people up. I realize the initial impression may be favorable; however, impressions can be deceiving and normally shed little light into the state of one's pantry. Believe me, I have met many individuals that seemed to really have their act together, only to find out that their pantries were a complete and utter mess. I include myself in this category, as there was a time that my pantry was depleted. It lacked all the good ingredients and any reserves to get me through. So I ask you, are you one of these individuals? By day do you seem to have everything together and by night you're just a train wreck? Are you proud of your inner pantry in life or do you have some serious work to do?

After my divorce, my inner pantry needed some major work. I was so one-dimensional in my approach to life that I had depleted my inner reserves. I was always giving to others and, as a result, I had little left for myself. This seems to happen a lot these days. In fact, I posted on my Facebook page the other day that I thought that most individuals had lost sight of what their true passion was in life. Needless to say, the response was overwhelming. There were many comments saying that the pace of life had pushed their passion down the priority list. In fact, one individual actually said that he was too busy helping others find their passion, so he had little time for his own. How sad is this? This is certainly an indication that our priorities are out of balance. We must strive to prioritize those activities or things that fill our cup or pantry. When we do, it benefits not only ourselves, but those around us. If we wish to foster the passion in others, we need to lead the way. For me it was art and creativity. In my younger years, I was heavily involved in art and photography. In my later years, I pushed this passion aside and, as a result, I received little in return. When I started to work on the state of my inner pantry, art and photography were just a few of the ingredients that I started to replenish. Once I started to head in the direction of stocking my inner pantry, those around me started to notice the renewed passion. The law of attraction started to kick in, and better people and better things started to enter into my life.

Your inner pantry is a reflection of your body of work, but it also must sustain the body of work of what's to come. Your pantry reflects the state of your reserves. If you constantly rob from the pantry, there soon will be nothing to rob from. The pantry must be in a constant state of replenishment. Just as it's critical for you to take care of yourself, to add the proper ingredients, it's equally important for you to maintain the state of your inner pantry. Your pantry drives the recipe for success. *Your pantry will get you through the times of both feast and famine. Be prepared—stock your pantry!*

Mott-Ohs

Never judge a book by its cover.

The door to the pantry can look very different than what's contained inside.

Put your best foot forward at all times, no matter what the circumstance.

Often in life, too much information is a bad thing.

Being selective with your words is truly one of the most valuable talents that you can acquire.

What you say is just as important as when you say it.

Time can either be your friend or your foe.

Your pantry will get you through the times of both feast and famine. Be prepared—stock your pantry!

CHAPTER 11

WHERE'S THE MEASURING CUP?

Look around you. Every day we live by measurements. We measure everything. How much do you weigh? Would you like one crème or two in your coffee? How do you feel today? How would you rate that movie last night? What is his approval rating? What is your GPA? Is the thermostat set at the ideal temperature? No matter what your circumstance, no matter where you are in life, measurement is a key factor in determining whether we are on track, satisfied, or meeting our goals.

Think back to your early childhood years. How many of you had that one doorway in the house that your mom or dad declared as the only place that you could write on the walls? In that very spot, your parents would carefully track your height measurements. With every inch, a new milestone, and, in turn, you were taught at a very early age that measure was important. However, don't you think that self-measurement has gotten a little out of hand? After all, it's one thing to want to be an inch taller or a year older. It's another thing to feel inferior to others due to a force-fed measurement. Who's to say how we should measure our own success?

So often we get caught up in measurements set by others. These measurements are not set by statistical or empirical data but rather are self-imposed. Go ahead, admit it. In walking down the street, you size up a person in a matter of seconds. You automatically form first impressions of people by how they carry themselves, how they dress, and how they act. These first impressions subconsciously are turned into measurements. We instantly hold up our measuring stick to determine how we compare. We are constantly trying to live up to the measurements set by others. Why, I ask you? Why are we so often striving to be like others? Why are we using the wrong measuring stick? I tend to believe that it's due to false perception. Society has fabricated a perception of what we have to be and need to have to be happy. Yes, it's created and then blasted across the information superhighway. People can't help but to be influenced by it. It's like a propaganda campaign aimed at those easily influenced by popular opinion. It's a war against self-determination, and self-determination is losing.

It's time that we threw the force-fed measuring stick away and set our own measurements for success. It's time for us all to live by our own stick! Allow me to clarify. Success applies to all things in life, big or small. Whether you are striving for a good grade in school, entering into a new relationship, or simply trying to lose a couple of pounds, it's imperative that you determine what your goals are and exactly what you wish to achieve. Once this is determined, it's easy to ascertain how much effort you will need to put forth. It truly needs to be your goal, your method, and your reward.

In the baking process, it's imperative that you put in the right ingredients, and in the proper quantities. *How well you follow the directions and how closely you adhere to the recommended measurements will dictate how successful you are in the end.* Use the proper amounts of ingredients and your success is a sure thing. Go rogue and use whatever you want and you're sure to have a mess on your hands. Have you ever heard the expression that too much of a good thing is a bad thing? In baking and in life, the same rules apply. Our lack of moderation can be disastrous! The optimal mix is what I like to call "Motteration." It's the ideal balance to achieve true success in life. Areas that lack Motteration are often areas that are either severely lacking or grossly overstated. This principle holds true in every aspect of your life. Spend too much time at work and your relationships are sure to suffer. Eat too much and your weight will begin to spike. Sleep less and decide to burn the candle at both ends and your energy levels and ability to focus will decline. *Achieve Motteration and life will gain the momentum you desire.* Life may not come with described measurements. However, through the process of trial and error, we often discover our path to happiness and the recipe for a healthy, balanced lifestyle. *Measurements are valuable tools when it comes to replicating success.* Once the ideal measurement is identified, it's up to us to maintain the balance and stick to the program.

Now that we have established that measurements can be both advantageous and detrimental, depending on their application, let's explore how they serve as points for pause and reflection during the baking process. Measurements can serve as rest stops through our journey of life. They serve as reminders of where we have come from and where we are going. If we are tackling a mountain and the only measurement of success is reaching the top, few will achieve success. Many will become frustrated when it comes to the length of the climb. However, if there are stopping points and increments of measure that are celebrated along the way, I guarantee the percentage for ultimate success will increase. Allow me to offer this example. As I was training for the Big Sur Marathon, I had been reading comments from runners who had completed the race. There were obviously some consistent themes, but one left a lasting impression. One runner wrote, *"Be sure to look back at certain points within the race, as the view of where you have just come from is just as or even more beautiful than the road forward."* It was true. With every turn and every hill, there was yet another breathtaking view to put in the memory banks. Every snapshot of where we had just come from was equally impressive. If I had failed to turn my head, if I had failed to pause and take it in, I would have missed those opportunities. The ability to look back in life and to celebrate incremental measurements during the process is one key ingredient to happiness and ultimate success.

Mott-Ohs

It's time that we threw the forced-fed measuring stick away and set our own measurements for success. It's time for us all to live by our own stick!

How well you follow the directions and how closely you adhere to the recommended measurements will dictate how successful you are in the end.

Achieve Motteration and life will gain the momentum you desire.

Measurements are valuable tools when it comes to replicating success.

"Be sure to look back at certain points within the race, as the view of where you have just come from is just as or even more beautiful than the road forward."

CHAPTER 12

YOU'RE PUTTING WHAT IN THE CUPCAKES?

When venturing from point A to point B, what's the normal course or path? Most would seek out directions to make it in the most efficient manner. However, if your mission was to enjoy the sites along the way, you might take a more scenic route. No matter what your goal, directions are always involved.

While baking, this idea holds true as well. Pick up any box of cupcake mix and you will find a detailed list of directions on the side of the box. Why? "To ensure success." Life would be one perfect cupcake if it always came with directions. The fact that it doesn't makes life a bit tricky. We are left to come up with our own recipe for success, one that is filled with all the proper ingredients. What is your recipe for success? What are your required ingredients? How much of each ingredient do you really need, and when is it necessary to mix them into the batter?

Every ingredient has its place. Every ingredient has its time. *An ingredient introduced at the wrong time could mean sure disaster for the end result.* Take a moment to think about all the ingredients that you need in life. Think about when each one should be mixed with other ingredients. Do you personally have all the ingredients to make the perfect batch in life?

Once you determine your personal recipe for success and happiness, you may notice that there are elements that exist that are not essential to the mix. Take, for instance, sardines. If someone told you to add a can of sardines to the cupcake mix, what would you do? You would probably make an awful face and declare that he or she was insane! How about some tobacco? Again, madness! Why would I purposely add an ingredient to the mix that I knew was sure to affect the outcome in a negative way? Sounds like an obvious question, yet we allow these unnecessary ingredients to be introduced all the time.

When these negative ingredients manifest as people in our lives, I like to refer to them as Sally Sardine and Tony Tobacco. Sally Sardine is constantly swimming around and, in her own way, stinking up the place. Sally is all about the negative, and her cup is always half empty. Tony Tobacco, on the other hand, is constantly fueling the fire. He's constantly searching for problems and, once found, blows on them to stoke the flames. He is a stoker; the hotter the fire, the better. He finds weakness and exploits it into terminal cancer. Both of these individuals feed on negativity and are normally surrounded by a sea of drama.

Most of you, at this point, are thinking of specific people that you know that resemble Sally and Tony. Since you have so quickly identified these individuals in your lives, now ask yourself, why have you allowed these folks to become part of your environment? Why have you allowed these folks to stink up your world or stoke the flames? Sometimes we don't realize how counterproductive these individuals are in the grand scheme of things. Sometimes we just dismiss them without grasping how much damage they leave in their wake. One thing's for sure: They are never part of the recipe for success. They will never be known as a positive ingredient that adds to that perfect batch of cupcakes.

The challenge is to identify these people and eliminate them from your life. Okay, let's be real. This is often easier said than done. Many of these people end up being family members or close friends that are not easily discarded or eliminated. However, identification is the key. Once you identify these folks as being either a sardine or tobacco, you can put them in their proper place. Their proper place is one of little consequence. Their proper place is not anywhere around you when you are trying to accomplish something of importance. David Russell, a famous classical guitarist, stated, "The hardest thing to learn in life is which bridge to cross and which to burn." Most people live by the motto of trying not to burn bridges. However, if the bridge is a one-way road leading to fire and turmoil, I say, "Burn, baby, burn!"

Make no mistake about it. *We are personally defined by those that surround us.* I am blessed with a great circle of friends. However, to be truly successful, we need to surround ourselves with more than just great friends. It's much like forming the perfect team at work or maybe even on the football field. You must identify key players for the skill positions and then those that are just there to cheer you to victory. In other words, when you analyze your recipe for success, you must size up your ingredients at the same time. Do I have enough cheerleaders, and do I have enough skilled team members?

Now that we recognize that people can either be positive or negative ingredients in our lives, let's dive a bit deeper. Let's investigate what I call "the dark side and the light side." Just as people can add or take away from your recipe for success, so too can material things. We introduce new ingredients into our lives all the time. With every new ingredient, there is a choice that we make. The choice just happens to be between the dark and the light sides.

Decisions fit into only two categories. They are either inconsequential or monumental. There is no middle ground. They can be as small as having a bite of a jelly doughnut to kick you off your diet or consciously deciding to abandon your core principles in life. They can initially seem to be of little consequence, and later, looking back, they were game changing. Decisions should not be taken lightly; they can be the catalyst for both positive and negative change. It only takes one spark to start a fire, one single snowball to start an avalanche, and, as I discussed earlier in the book, a kind gesture to start a movement of goodwill. *One pebble thrown into a pond is far reaching through its never-ending ripples.*

We often introduce negative ingredients into our lives, as they seem to bring us short-term happiness or quench an immediate craving. They can often appear to be gray in nature. Gray area items are those that are easily misconstrued. They often appear good on the outside but are snowballs or sparks that lead to the personal misdirection in life. Listen up, folks. *When we're talking about the recipe for success, there is no middle ground. There is no gray area. It's black or white, dark or light, and there is no in between.* If it appears to be gray, I can guarantee that it's merely a disguise for the dark side. If it has a spin to it, it's bound to fall over at some point.

We, as Americans, take in so much garbage that it's truly not a wonder why we are in the midst of an identity crisis. We don't know who we are and we have depleted all of our natural resources. We are constantly relying on artificial substances to pick us up in the morning and to place us in a state of rest in the evening. These stimulants and depressants are taking us for a roller-coaster ride. One minute, we are soaring to the sky and the other we are crashing down to earth. It's these short-term fixes that are paving the way to the dark side.

To be truly successful in any area of your life, whether it's finances, relationships, health, or your spiritual well-being, you must add the right ingredients. If you are constantly adding garbage to the mixture, all you will get in return is nothing short of a mess. So ask yourselves this question: what kind of negative ingredients am I either consciously or unconsciously adding to the mix right now? Then make the commitment to distance yourself or eliminate those elements from your baking process. Is it smoking, overeating, lack of exercise, drug abuse, irresponsible spending, caffeine, burning the candle at both ends, or lack of attention and effort in your relationships? No matter what the poor ingredient, you must take drastic and immediate measures to eliminate it from the equation. Why? Because it is not part of the ideal mix. One bad choice normally leads to a string of bad, just as the spark began a fire and the snowball started an avalanche. Make the choice today. Make the right choice today. It's your batch. Make it happen!

Mott-Ohs

An ingredient introduced at the wrong time could mean sure disaster to the end result.

We are personally defined by those that surround us.

The dark side can plummet us into the depths of depravity and despair, while the light side can lead us to the light of success, wealth, and eternal happiness.

One pebble thrown into a pond is far reaching through its never-ending ripples.

When we're talking about the recipe for success, there is no middle ground. There is no gray area. It's black or white, dark or light, and there is no in between.

CHAPTER 13

A PINCH OF ENTHUSIASM GOES A LONG WAY

Every day, as you wake up and your feet hit the floor, do you ever feel like it's the same old routine? "Same stuff, different day." You have the power to change this at any given moment. Just as in the baking process, if you use the same ingredients over and over, the cupcake is bound to look and taste the same every time. If you simply switch up the ingredients, it can have a measurable or even drastic effect. It's as easy as taking a right turn versus a left, two totally different directions, and I guarantee a different experience and result.

I like to think, *"Sometimes you just need to change your way to work."* For example, I had been taking the same route to work for months. Same series of rights, same series of lefts, and even stopping at the same coffee shop for the same cup of coffee every morning. When I stuck to a norm of hitting the snooze button two to three times and keeping my shower to seven minutes, I realized that as I entered the coffee shop, I was seeing the same people. It was like a group of items on the same conveyer belt. We all looked the same, headed in the same direction, and, for the most part, acted the same each morning. It's amazing how we adopt routines and stick to them. Then we suddenly wake up. When we do, we wonder why we're in a rut; stuck on the eternal conveyer belt of life with no end. Even more amazing is that we fail to realize that these routines affect how we start our days and how we feel about ourselves. *Are we setting ourselves up for success through the routines that we follow?* Think about it! Are you constantly rushing around in the morning because you fail to give yourself the proper time? Does this set your day off in a flurry and the rest of day just follows suit? Are there things that you can do to change the situation? Certainly! It might be as easy as accomplishing one or two tasks the night before to save that five or ten minutes of prep time in the morning. It may be going to bed an hour earlier to wake up more prepared for the day. There's a plethora of possible options within your control. You have license to be creative with your own life. You simply need to commit!

For all you parents who struggle to get yourself and your kids ready, it's like a never-ending battle against time. We often find ourselves on the losing end of the finish line. *What is stopping you from gaining the competitive edge?* Maybe it's your perception. Maybe you honestly believe that to gain the upper hand, it takes a feat of greatness beyond your grasp. To that I say, "You are wrong!" Most of the time, the solution is as easy as one, two, three. As with the previous example, it could be just as easy as setting all the kids' clothes out the night before. It could be as easy as packing their lunch boxes the day before. It could be as easy as ensuring that all their homework is completed and backpacks are sitting at the front door ready to hit the road in the morning. Yes, these simple steps can mean the difference between a positive or negative start to your day. Rushing or even being late will, without a doubt, send you into a never-ending tailspin for the rest of the day.

In my case, I was visiting the same coffee shop every morning. I realized that I was running into the same people. I was destined to have the same experience. Through my actions, I was creating a self-imposed sense of déjà vu. So one day, *I decided to alter my course, to change the morning routine, to take a left instead of a right, just to see if the outcome would be different.* I ended up at the same coffee shop chain, but a different store in a different location. Now, let me preface this by saying that the customer service at my old coffee shop was always good. As I entered this new coffee shop—again, same chain, but yet different location—I quickly realized the difference between good and great. Something was different. Within thirty seconds, I was greeted or touched in some fashion by two or three employees who were "morning people." You know these people. These people are fueled by the a.m. rather than the p.m. They are the sun worshipers, those who spring out of bed at the crack of dawn and meet the day with a self-infused vigor. These folks are definitely packin' sunshine. :-) The store manager had hired the right people for the job. What is most important, they had received amazing training when it came to altering the experience of their customers. *They were taught that even before I was given my first shot of caffeine, they alone had the power to give me an additional morning boost.*

Something was different. They invested time and training into their people. They executed a plan to market the experience rather than just the product. The ingredients were totally different, and the end result was amazing. As I walked out of the coffee shop, I felt totally pumped! I had an everlasting smile on my face and it had little to do with my mocha. It had everything to do with the experience. *Enthusiasm and sincerity are contagious*, and this store and its employees and managers really got this idea. They did a great job of pointing my day in the right direction. They truly had their sprinkles! By this point, I should have the attention of anyone in management, sales, customer service, or marketing. This is truly the difference between good and great.

I will never forget that experience. It was a day that opened my eyes to how just *the littlest of things can make the biggest difference in how you jump-start your day or life.* This was a CPA, compound positive ascent, as we have discussed in a previous chapter. It's imperative that we recognize their existence. They are truly that first step that starts the climb to a better place in life. *Once we learn to recognize the start of the compound positive ascent, we can truly harness the power behind them.*

Haven't you ever had one of those days where everything just seems to be going your way? You literally walk away from the day saying, "Wow, that was the best day ever! If only I could replicate that." Imagine if you could harness the power of the CPA to make it not only happen for the day, but to stretch the wave of positive energy on for a week, a month, or even a year. If so, I am sure you would jump at the chance. Well, I am here to tell you that you can. *With knowledge comes power, and as we gain more knowledge, we get stronger as individuals. True wisdom comes when we choose to use the knowledge and experience to better ourselves and those around us.* The knowledge and awareness allows you to harness the power of the CPA. This gives you the competitive advantage!

Although I truly believe that my parents were some of the best teachers, I sometimes look back and wish that they had taught me more. Maybe it was part of the grand plan for me to learn on my own. If so, that's fine. But I believe I would have benefited more if they had jump-started that learning process. As a result, whether my kids like it or not, whether they choose to listen or turn their heads, I have decided to pass along as many of my life's lessons as possible. The other day my youngest son, Hayden, who is fourteen, called me to ask how one of my motivational speeches went that day. I was pleasantly surprised that he took the time to reach out. It's a rare thing to see in a teen these days, as they are often secluded and self-consumed. It says a lot. I told him I had some areas of improvement that I needed to focus on before my next speech. His response was. "Baby steps, Dad...baby steps!" I laughed out loud. After ending the call with him, it made me think about how much kids listen without acknowledging it. As parents, we wonder if what we say is ever doing any good or not. It's moments like these that serve as confirmation that my words didn't fall on deaf ears. *So, to all you parents out there, keep talking, keep walking, and keep teaching. Your kids are watching, listening, and are sure to follow in your footsteps!* Make sure that *you* leave footprints leading down the path you would like them to follow.

Since I've covered Hayden, my youngest, it's now time to give Kaley, my fifteen-year-old daughter, some airtime. Kaley is a wonderful young girl who is blossoming into a woman. Oh yes, this is a polite and politically correct way of saying she is a teenager. For all you parents out there, you know from where I speak. Teens are the ultimate agers! I swear that every grey hair on my head is directly linked to the difficulties that come with parenting teens. Despite their downside, we forever love them, and I am dedicated to seeing them through this period and welcoming the time when they become human again.☺

Kaley came to me recently and she was beaming with excitement. At the ripe old age of fifteen, she had just landed her first job interview with Baskin-Robbins. For those of you who might have not had the pleasure of ever visiting a Baskin-Robbins, it just happens to be the home of thirty-one flavors of ice cream. It's one of the only ice cream establishments that have survived the test of time. Yes, it survived the yogurt craze, the carbohydrate famine, and, in the end, Baskin-Robbins is still going strong. What a great first opportunity Kaley had sitting in front of her. I obviously joined in her excitement and firmly planted myself in her corner. After ending the phone call, I realized that even though she was excited, her nerves were starting to get the best of her. What does a fifteen-year-old know about getting a job or even going through the interview process? She had every reason to be nervous. As her nerves were racing, my mind was racing just as fast, but with great ideas of how I could best help in her pursuit to become the Queen of Thirty-One Flavors.

As I was thinking about all the wisdom that I could bestow, I quickly realized that I needed to be tactical in my delivery. If there was one thing that I had learned through parenting teens, it's that it's very difficult to tell them what to do or offer advice that will sink in to their know-it-all brains. When dealing with teens, it's essential to be more creative so that they believe your advice is their own. This one idea may just apply to all ages. On that note, I decided that rather than telling her how to get prepared for the interview, I was going to show her.

So I started down the path of showing rather than telling. I called Kaley and scheduled to pick her up and take her to a late lunch after school. As she jumped in the car, I explained that rather than going to lunch, we were going to eat ice cream, and lots of it! We were going on a mission to shop three different ice cream stores, including the one where she had applied for the job. I explained that we would be sampling their products and, more importantly, rating them on customer service and presentation. Yes, I quickly received that "Dad, you are nuts!" look, but at the same time I also received this really cool look, like "You are so cool for doing this with me, but I am too cool as a teenager to ever tell you that." So, I handed her the following list and explained that it was her job to rate the ice cream establishments on the following:

- ☐ Were you greeted by a smile and a welcome when you entered the door?
- ☐ Was the sales associate dressed to impress?
- ☐ Was the sales associate enthusiastic?
- ☐ Were you promptly served?
- ☐ If you weren't promptly served, did the sales associate apologize for the wait?
- ☐ Did the sales associate try to upsell you?
- ☐ Did the sales associate thank you and ask you to come again?
- ☐ Did you receive a receipt and the proper amount of change for your transaction?
- ☐ Was the establishment clean and inviting?
- ☐ Were the products displayed in an easy-to-find and orderly fashion?

As I said before, with teens especially, *if you walk them through the process rather than telling them, you are more apt to leave a lasting impression.* Again, this might just apply to any age. As we toured the three different establishments, I could see Kaley's facial expressions change during the sales process as the sales associates were either hitting every point or not hitting them at all. Kaley got to see firsthand the impact of positive and negative sales skills on the customer. This was such a valuable lesson to learn. How are you to get in the head and manipulate the experience of the customer if you have never been one yourself?

As the afternoon progressed and my appetite for ice cream diminished, we hit the final ice cream establishment. I had purposely planned that it would be the Baskin-Robbins at which Kaley had applied. I had saved Baskin-Robbins for last, as I wanted Kaley to have had some time to think about the questions. I wanted her to be extremely critical when it came to rating the customer service at her prospective place of employment. Much to our surprise, the sales associate nailed all of our questions and left us rating the store above all the rest.

As Kaley was writing down her notes from our last visit, I told her that we were off to one more location. She asked me eagerly, "Where to next, Dad?" I then explained that we were off to the stationery store to pick up a thank-you card. It was to hand deliver to the manager shortly after her interview. I explained to Kaley that the interview process was much like the sales process. *The ultimate goal is to leave a lasting impression on the individual that you are attempting to impress.* I confidently assured her that after she handed the store manager a copy of her customer service survey results and conveyed all the things that she had learned through the process, she would be steps ahead of any competition vying for the same job. In addition, she would be leaving a lasting and sincere impression on the store manager by following up in a prompt manner with a hand-written thank-you card.

What lessons had I taught Kaley in a matter of hours? I had taught her the basic principles of marketing, sales, customer service, and follow-up that I had learned through a series of jobs over the course of weeks, months, and in some cases years. More specifically, I had showed her the following:

- How to control the sales process from the very beginning.
- Enthusiasm sells.
- You instill confidence by looking presentable and organized.
- Prompt attention shows respect.
- It's important to be thorough.
- Sincerity will set you apart from the rest.
- Preparation is the key to success.
- Follow-through will seal the deal.
- When you do all of these, it's hard not be successful, and first time customers will become repeat customers.

At the end of this process she was still nervous. It was still her first interview. However, she had a new sense of confidence. *With confidence comes empowerment.* Rather than telling her how important being prepared was, I showed her. She saw the proof in the pudding. *When confronted with a challenging situation in life, your best offense is an arsenal filled with a plethora of preparation.*

When in your life have you been nervous or apprehensive about something? Maybe it was a big presentation, your first day at a new job, or possibly a test in school. No matter what the circumstance, I guarantee that the outcome will always be better when you are, one, prepared, and two, when you add some sprinkles to your effort. "Sprinkles," you say? Yes, that extra energy that shows you hold yourself to a higher standard. You are willing to give that extra effort in life that makes all the difference. *After all, a pinch of enthusiasm goes a long way!* The moral of story is, Kaley got the job and she is now the Queen of Thirty-One Flavors. What is more important, she is what I call a "sprinkle pusher!" She is constantly trying to upsell her customers on adding sprinkles to their order. I find it highly amusing that she is pushing the same thing in her career as I am in mine.

Life is competitive. No matter what you're doing, there will always be certain internal and external pressures that will give you that opportunity to stand out. Whether you decide to buy into that idea or not, it's best to set yourself apart in the world. The goal is to not morph into just an ordinary cupcake—one that can be bought anywhere, one that is defined by mediocrity. You must accept the fact that you are one of a kind. You are truly special. There is no other like you on the face of the planet. Once you realize and accept this fact, you become unique. You become special. This acceptance is truly the largest step in finding your sprinkles in life.

Mott-Ohs

Sometimes you just need to change your way to work.

Are we setting ourselves up for success through the routines that we follow?

What's stopping you from gaining the competitive edge?

I decided to alter my course, to change the morning routine, to take a left instead of a right, just to see if the outcome would be different.

They were taught that even before I was given my first shot of caffeine, they alone had the power to give me an additional morning boost.

Enthusiasm and sincerity are contagious.

The littlest of things can make the biggest difference in how you jump-start your day or life.

Once we learn to recognize the start of the compound positive ascent, we can truly harness the power behind it.

With knowledge comes power, and as we gain more knowledge, we get stronger as individuals. True wisdom comes when we choose to use the knowledge and experience to better ourselves and those around us.

Teens are the ultimate agers!

If you walk them through the process rather than telling them, you are more apt to leave a lasting impression.

The ultimate goal is to leave a lasting impression on the individual that you are attempting to impress.

With confidence comes empowerment.

When confronted with a challenging situation in life, your best offense is an arsenal filled with a plethora of preparation.

CHAPTER 14

LET'S MIX IT UP!

We've already talked about balance in life. Now I'd like to expand on the subject. Have you ever felt like there's just not enough of you to go around? How can I ever be everything to everyone? If you are relating right now, it's probably because you haven't developed the art of saying no. Are you a yes man? Do you have trouble saying no when asked to say yes? If you answered yes, you've just proven my point, and you are probably a people pleaser—an individual who feels like his or her sole purpose is to serve others. You are someone who defines your self-worth by serving others before yourself. It's called being altruistic. Altruism is defined as "the selfless concern for the welfare of others." It's a traditional virtue in many cultures, and a building block of various religious traditions. In most cases, having this virtue in life is a worthy pursuit. However, if this pursuit is all consuming, it can be counterproductive to achieving balance and the right mixture. If you are this individual, you are probably scratching your head. You're trying to figure out how to fulfill the desire to serve while also serving yourself. How do I accomplish both? *The goal needs to be to take care of others at the same time as you are taking care of numero uno.* Yes, *you* are number one!

Balance is the key to everything in life. Imagine the mechanics of a wheel. You have the hub that exists in the center, which holds the entire thing together. Then you have the spokes that emanate from the hub and connect at the outermost points of the rim. The rim is where the rubber hits the road.

All of these components work hand in hand together to achieve balance, which ultimately translates into forward momentum. Face it. We're all about forward momentum. Everyone is trying to get somewhere, normally too fast, to try to achieve something.

Where do you picture yourself in the schematics of a wheel? Are you the hub that holds everything together? Are you the spokes that strengthen the process? Or are you the rim and rubber, where the speed happens? *Whichever role you decide to play, you have to admit, without strength in all areas, you will go nowhere fast.* This is where the balance begins. *It's imperative that you realize and admit to yourself that you're stronger as a collective. The support system that you choose to build around yourself will define your ultimate success.* Conversely, if you choose to surround yourself with negative influences, your life is sure to take a wrong turn. Your wheel is sure to weaken.

Think of yourself as a wheel avoiding potholes. Potholes ruin forward momentum. They make the process hazardous and can often do major damage to your wheel. What are your potholes? Potholes can be people, circumstances, or vices that stand in your way. Are you a smoker? If so, I venture to guess that your smoking is a pothole in the way of becoming healthy. Are you addicted to credit cards? If so, then I bet those double-digit interest rates are serving as a pothole in the way of true financial stability. In your job, are you one of those people who focus on the negative or blame everything on circumstances around you? If so, then I bet that this negative attitude and lack of accountability are serving as a pothole standing in the way of that true promotion that you desire. Every spoke of your wheel can represent someone or something in your kitchen. Each spoke adds an essential ingredient. The more emphasis that you place on the strength of your collective wheel, the more successful you will become in life.

To further this point, think of yourself as the hub. Everything is designed to work around you. Often when we think of this, we think of having to carry the entire load. It's the opposite. If you take care of your spokes, the weight ends up being evenly distributed. Each spoke is playing its part. It's only when you don't pay attention to some of the spokes that they weaken. When they weaken, the whole wheel is in jeopardy of incurring serious damage. The integrity of your wheel is compromised.

Let's take time to clearly identify what ingredients we need in life to be truly content. What ingredients do we personally need to be truly successful by our own definition? Below is a diagram of what I like to call "Mottivation Power Wheel." You may find a blank copy of this wheel at www.mottivation.com under the training section of my Web site. As you will see in the following example, I have specified different areas as priorities in life. I then ranked them on a scale of one to ten (ten being the best). For each of you, these areas will be different. Take time to fill out your personal power wheel today and rank how you feel currently about each spoke. Be honest, as this will truly point you in the right direction when it comes to strengthening your own personal position in life.

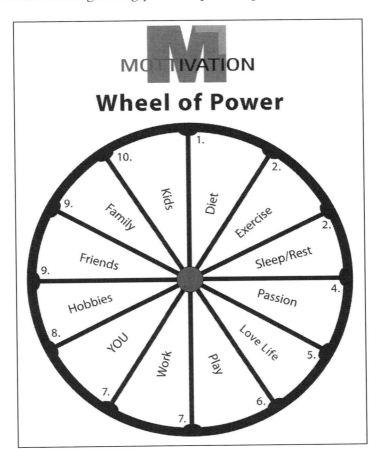

Once you have identified all the key ingredients and ratings encompassed in your power wheel, it's now time to set priorities. Yes, priorities, as I have explained in a previous chapter. It's essential to find our cracks and dig down to where our foundation is compromised the most. Anything short of repairing our foundation is simply a waste of time and effort. We do this by applying what I like to call "the pothole test" to the power wheel assessment. In the following diagram of a pothole, you can clearly see how we have transferred the above ratings on the power wheel into our own personal pothole. You can see how our lowest ratings on our wheel translate into our deepest areas for concern in our foundation. We must attack these areas before we attack anything else. When we do, we strengthen our foundation and all improvements to come will be long lasting.

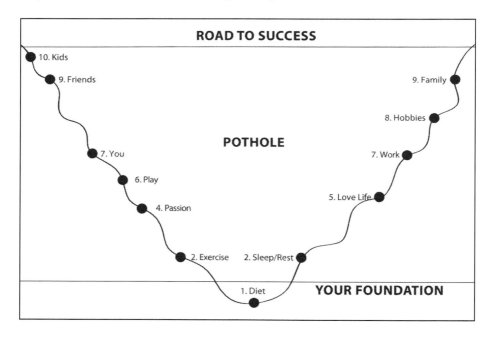

Once you identify your pothole priorities, you can implement the same power wheel assessment for each spoke of the wheel. Again, start with your weakest spoke. Simply make the individual spoke the hub of a wheel. Then identify all the key ingredients that you must have in place to realize success in that one area. Rate them again, apply the pothole test to that specific area, and you are well on your way to correcting any deficient area of your life. You are well on your way to strengthening your wheel. Momentum is soon to be yours.

In the right proportion, once all the ingredients are in the wheel, it's time to mix it up. Proportions are important. Just imagine if the baker was blindfolded, had no measuring cup, and was left to feel his way around the kitchen. How do you imagine the cupcakes would turn out? Would the mixture resemble batter? Would you want to be the guinea pig in that taste test? I don't think so! What kind of state do you think the kitchen would be in after the baker got done? Have you ever felt like your life resembles a blindfolded disaster? Maybe it's time to open your eyes. Maybe it's time to take the blindfold off.

Once you determine the right ingredients and measurements, it's just as essential to determine when the ingredients are to be used in the mixing process. Just as in life, everything has its own time and place. You may have heard the expression "We will serve no wine before its time." Well, this premise holds true to the baking process. Ingredients introduced at the wrong time are met with resistance. They tend to ruin the recipe or just simply don't mix in well. The same is true in life. Can you imagine trying to send a first grader to college? How well would that go over? For many reasons, it wouldn't. The child is too immature, and he or she simply wouldn't be ready from an educational standpoint. Can you imagine what a cupcake would end up looking like if that same blindfolded baker was to add the sprinkles, icing, and the eggs all at once? What if he just skipped the mixing step all together? It would be a disaster. It wouldn't resemble the traditional cupcake. That's for sure!

We know now that we must have the proper ingredients. We know that each ingredient has its own specified amount and, just as important, we know when it's introduced into the process. So let's discuss the mixing process for a bit. *In life, motion is the key to everything. With motion we gain momentum, and with momentum we gain velocity. Success comes when you achieve positive velocity.* Every positive motion in life has its own equally important windup. Think of a golfer and his backswing. Before the golfer swings at the ball, there is a very deliberate backswing. It's the setup for the forward motion. Much like the ingredients, there are certain mechanical elements that must be mixed together to produce a proper backswing. They must be executed in a particular order to ensure success. Once the swing occurs and contact is made, the clubface must achieve the perfect contact with the ball. This perfect contact is the end product of a proper backswing. As a result, the ball ends up going in the desired direction and gains the proper velocity to be considered a successful golf shot.

When in life have you hit a great shot? When in life have you sent a golf ball soaring into the trees and out of play? Think back to these times. Think about the motions that were in play leading up to the success or the disaster. Were you a positive contributor to ensure that all the ingredients were in place? Was the backswing or the mixture the catalyst for the successful end result? In the case of the out-of-play golf ball, were you a negative contributor? Were you lacking the right ingredients? Were you lacking the proper timing to ensure a successful result?

The mixing process is one that strives to accomplish the right consistency and the perfect mix leading into the baking process. Much like in life, if there is too much of one thing or something is introduced at the wrong time, it's like oil and water. They just don't mix.

Mott-Ohs

The goal needs to be to take care of others at the same time as you are taking care of numero uno.

Whichever role you decide to play, you have to admit, without strength in the other areas, you will go nowhere fast.

It's imperative that you realize and admit to yourself that you're stronger as a collective. The support system that you choose to build around yourself will define your ultimate success.

The keys that we don't use all the time, but yet keep around, only seem to weigh us down and add that unnecessary clutter to our lives.

In life, motion is the key to everything. With motion we gain momentum, and with momentum we gain velocity. Success comes when you achieve positive velocity.

CHAPTER 15

TIMER'S SET, NOW WALK AWAY

A ll the prep work is done, cupcakes are in the oven, and the timer's set. Now, what should we do? Most of us have grown accustomed to a fast-paced lifestyle, go, go, go! We're constantly trying to cram the most into every minute. We have developed the ability to multitask. *My idea of multitasking is lying down, falling into a deep sleep, having an awesome dream, snoring, and waking up reenergized. That's my idea of multitasking!*

We're all born with the innate ability to multitask. One of the simplest things that we do when we multitask is to breathe. We are known as unconscious breathers. This means that we don't need to be conscious to breathe. No matter what we're doing, awake or asleep, our body knows that it must breathe to survive. In the same respect, our bodies must have sleep. Our body will tell us when we're tired, and we must listen. If we aren't good listeners, we end up sleep deprived. Sleep deprivation is extremely hazardous to our health. It can inhibit our ability to function properly. When we deprive ourselves of the proper ingredients, our concentration levels drop, and memory becomes impaired. Our ability to perform simple tasks diminishes and we struggle to rationalize. *Small speed bumps become insurmountable mountains in the sleep-deprived mind.* So I ask you: why would you choose to be a bad listener when your body is talking? If your body was to say breathe, you would breathe. If your body is asking for sleep, why would you choose to deprive yourself of the ingredients that are essential to living healthy?

Why would you choose to add the following side effects associated with sleep deprivation to your life?

* Depression
* Heart disease
* Hypertension
* Irritability
* Slower reaction times
* Slurred speech
* Tremors

I believe that we stop listening to our bodies as our bodily constraints sometimes stand in the way of accomplishing our goals in life. "I don't have time to rest." "There is not enough time in the day." "If only there could be two of me, then I might get everything accomplished." If only we could be more like dolphins or whales. Dolphins or whales? Yes, dolphins and whales are mammals just like us. They need to sleep and breathe at the same time. However, the last time I checked, there were very few whale and dolphin bed and breakfasts in the deep blue sea. So, what do they do? It's a proven fact that dolphins and whales sleep while they are awake. They shut down half of their brain for periods of time to get the necessary amount of sleep. They routinely sleep eight hours. Is it that dolphins and whales have determined that eight hours is the ideal amount of sleep each day? I don't think so. I believe that the natural order of things has instilled this as a preprogrammed protection device. Now stop that! I know what you are thinking. "If only I could sleep and stay awake at the same time, I would get so much accomplished." That's the wrong train of thought. Dolphins and whales have adapted to their surroundings to maintain a healthy lifestyle. They must accomplish both; otherwise, they would drown. If we attempt to adapt by not sleeping, it will only result in overwork and a state of depletion.

As we grow older, we eventually move out of the house. Mom and Dad are no longer around to enforce a routine bedtime. Why do you suppose a routine bedtime was enforced? Was it because your parents were sick and tired of dealing with you? Did they desperately need some downtime to recover from the hell that you put them through? These reasons may have some validity.

However, I think that there was a deeper motive at play. Your parents, being wise adults, knew that *in order for you to have a productive tomorrow, it was essential for you to obtain the proper rest today.*

I remember my kids when I would stretch them past their designated bedtime. It was like an alien being had entered their bodies. One minute they were fine, and the next, their heads were spinning 360 degrees, all while spitting pea soup across the room. For those of you that don't recognize the reference, it's from the movie *The Exorcist.* Possessed by the devil, the character portrayed by the actress Linda Blair sat on the bed as her head turned completely around. While doing so, she was spitting pea soup all over the room. Lack of sleep seems much like being possessed. Rash actions can be traced to sleep-deprived, irrational thinking. It's hard enough to rationalize with a child in the best of circumstances. Throw in sleep deprivation and the party's over. Yes, it's extremely difficult to control children as they are growing from stage to stage. However, it's compounded when they haven't obtained the proper amount of sleep.

As adults, imagine if you still had a bedtime. Think about what really happens after 10 p.m. I'm here to tell you, nothing good happens after that hour. Many of you would disagree, as there's a laundry list of things that happen after 10 p.m. It's your quiet time, time to catch up on must-see television, time to have one-on-one time with your significant other, but it's also the time that most people turn on the television and the midnight snack attack occurs. It's been said that if you simply consume three hundred calories after dinner for a month's time, you will gain an additional thirty pounds a year. If you're shaking your head in disbelief, consider the following scientific facts: Leptin is the hormone in the human body that affects our feelings of fullness and satisfaction. Ghrelin is the hormone in the body that stimulates the appetite. Combine these two hormones, which happens as a result of sleep deprivation (leptin levels falling and ghrelin levels climbing), and you end up feeling hungrier without feeling satisfied. It's the perfect recipe for overeating and a sure-fire road map to obesity.

Thanks to modern technology, any late-night television missed as a result of an early bedtime can now be recorded and watched during reasonable hours.

Those late-night cravings for food that you would normally resist would be circumvented by sleep. Late-night alone time with your significant other can be replaced with a morning workout together. The morning workout will then lead to a higher level of intimacy and passion after the new routine is established. It's a proven fact that your level of physical fitness affects, one, your sex drive, and two, how you are perceived sexually in the eyes of your partner. Any late-night work will be accomplished during the day with your renewed level of energy. Frantic activities, normally the precursor to a restless night, can now be replaced with more soothing activities that serve as foreplay to a restful night. This restful night leaves you totally reenergized and ready to attack the next day.

In a recent ABC News/*Washington Post* poll, 61 percent of Americans said the economy is causing stress in their lives; one-third said the stress is "serious." Even though we realize that our current position is serious at best, we still seem to feel as if we must make the most of every minute. "Carpe diem, seize the day!" "Life is too short to waste." As much as there are positive lessons to be learned from these phrases, they are also two-sided coins. These ideas have a tendency to create the belief that we must accomplish something every waking minute. Before you know it, if you're not multitasking and sucking the marrow out of life, you're feeling guilty. Admit it. How many of you have felt guilty sitting around when there was something else yet to accomplish? I have news: the list will always be there.

Who's to say that you aren't accomplishing something by doing just one thing at a time? Who's to say that you aren't achieving something by just staging down? I never was a great math student. However, I can do this simple calculation: if you're trying to accomplish four tasks at once, and you give them 25 percent of your effort versus giving one task 100 percent, the end result is still 100 percent on both sides of the equation. Some may even argue that you were more productive focusing on the single task, as you were more mindful and present. Those that focus on a single task are less prone to mistakes or missteps requiring elements to be redone.

Life's a marathon, not a sprint. It's filled with uphill climbs, flat sections, and downhill speedways. All of these stages have their distinct purpose and need individual attention to maneuver them effectively.

The uphill sections are there to strengthen you. They are harder than the others. We often view these challenging, turbulent times as ones that we would just rather forget. In looking back on them, after all the dust settles, they're often the times when we learn the most about ourselves. We tend to find our inner strength. We often find our true friends and support system. Those who are true to you seem to stand up and rally in times of crisis. Those who are not quietly step back into the shadows. These are truly the times when you find whether you have the right mix of people around you.

The flat sections are there for endurance. These sections are where you really start to log the miles. This is the section that tests your longevity. The flats are not a sprint, but rather a time to accomplish a lot at a very steady pace. They are also the times in which you can conserve energy for the downhill sprints and uphill climbs. Often our biggest accomplishments are achieved within the flat sections. College degrees, longer relationships, tenure at work, and just the accomplishment of running a marathon, as I did, can be viewed as major achievements. These accomplishments can only be attained through tenacious fortitude over the long haul. Not everything needs to be a quick touchdown to be viewed as a success. Sometimes the longer it takes to accomplish the achievement, the higher that people raise it on the pedestal.

The downhill speedways are there to cover ground quickly. We have all witnessed it. Life throws you deadlines, and it's one big sprint to the end. Time to beat the deadline. Often some people do their best work in this stage. There are those individuals who thrive under pressure. This is the stage where you give it your all for a limited duration. The individuals who try to maintain this pace for long normally end up crashing. Nobody can maintain the sprint continuously throughout the marathon.

It's okay not to be going twenty-four/seven. In most cases, it's essential to break the day up into diverse and manageable sections. For all you full-time caregivers out there, my ex-spouse used to say, "I bust my butt all day taking care of the kids, cleaning house, making meals, and being a social coordinator. At the end of the day, I'm simply too tired to do anything else or be anything more to anyone." Sound familiar? Yes, this is the classic case of how too much of anything becomes detrimental. *When one person is carrying the entire load, it will always have adverse effects on a relationship.* On the other hand, the full-time breadwinners are saying, "I work all day. If my income goes away, the entire thing will fall down like a weak house of cards. The stressors involved in being the sole breadwinner in the family are more than you can imagine." Both points are valid. However, we're missing the most important piece of the puzzle. Just like in the baking process, it's essential to have the proper ingredients, but, even more important, it's essential to move away from the oven at times. In other words, if one person in a relationship carries the sole burden of one part of the partnership, it will take its toll. *The solution is to release each other from what's all consuming.* Allow each other to recharge the batteries through variety and, most important, through downtime. That downtime is the baking stage. After measuring, mixing, and finally placing the batch in the oven, you have time to kick your heels up and enjoy the comforting aroma of the cupcakes beginning to bake.

Life always throws us opportunities for downtime. It's normally just a matter of whether we choose to seize them or not. Often we don't recognize these opportunities. We are so busy that we fail to interpret the signs, or we just aren't listening. Take, for instance, the step in the baking process that states, "Bake at 350 degrees for 45 minutes." Many will interpret this as "I have 45 minutes before I need to be back here. Otherwise, they will get burned." Others might interpret it as, "I have 45 minutes to cram as much into my life as humanly possible." Others won't trust the directions and will return to the oven repeatedly, as they are afraid something will happen if they are not watching.

In business, this person is labeled as the overcontrolling and possessive micromanager. This individual never lets things go. He or she never delegates responsibility. He or she never reaches that stage of true productivity and balance. These micromanagers are doomed to live a life of mediocrity. Who do you know around you that has no faith in the process? Yes, you need to have faith. At some point, you have to trust your preparation enough to take you through the baking stage. Simply put the cupcakes in the oven and walk away with the comforting knowledge that your preparation was thorough and flawless. Have you ever heard the saying "A watched pot never boils?" I like to think that the person who coined the phrase truly got this idea. Bake at 350 for 45 minutes: it's an opportunity to savor the time.

I recently drove my oldest son, Jordan, across the country to attend Penn State. It was a tremendous opportunity. We took our time traveling across the country. I purposely turned what could have been a sprint into a ten-day marathonlike adventure. It was an adventure that was literally filled with hills, flats, and downhill sections. There were parts of the trip that were over-the-top exciting, such as river rafting in Colorado and visiting the Pro Football Hall of Fame in Canton, Ohio.

On the flip side, there were some really dull and monotonous sections, like the salt flats of Utah and the never-ending cornfields of Kansas. As we were navigating through and across this very diverse landscape, I couldn't help but draw a correlation between our journey and the previous eighteen years of his childhood. The journey of growing up had been just as diverse. Some good and some bad, but regardless, we had both arrived at the same spot, at the same time, facing the same opportunity. Much like the baking process, we had assembled all the proper ingredients, mixed it up in a great big bowl, poured it into cupcake tins, and were traveling to put it in the oven.

As I was about ready to throw my son into the oven of college, I had this over-whelming urge to bestow my final words of never-ending advice. For those of you who know me, you know that to have a trapped audience at 70 mph for ten days is truly a mouthwatering opportunity. I contemplated talking even if he was sleeping in the hopes that some subliminal messages might permeate that thick skull. In the end, I decided to take my own advice. I knew that all the ingredients were there. Everything that his mother and I had taught took years of preparation, measuring, and mixing. Rather than preaching or lecturing across the country, I embraced the opportunity to strengthen the bond that he and I now have as adults. I decided to reinforce all the proper ingredients by showing him again how I surround myself with them. Never did we push too hard across the country to the point that it put our health or well-being in jeopardy. We ran and worked out across the country. We met with some great people with whom I surround myself. Rather than preaching to him, I asked each one of them to offer up some words of advice as he was standing on the threshold of independence. The following are some of the sage words offered:

- ☐ "Find your true passion."
- ☐ "Learn to understand people."
- ☐ "Don't ever get caught without a plan B."
- ☐ "Take risks."
- ☐ "Stay close to what you love."
- ☐ "If you always do what you have always done, you will always get what you have always gotten."
- ☐ "Follow your moral compass."

These were just some of the highlights. Jordan got to see how positive relationships, born through the years, had survived the test of time and were still worthy of my attention and energy. It was an amazing experience and one I will never forget. My sincere thanks go out to all with whom we stayed during our journey across the country. You know who you are, and it wasn't by chance that we chose to spend time with you. Rather, it was a very calculated stop to allow those that have been instrumental in my personal growth to rub off on Jordan as he was about to face this exciting and challenging time in his life.

When it came time to let him bake at 350 for four years, I simply hugged him, told him that I loved him, and turned and walked away. As I'm writing this section, I'm on a plane flying three thousand miles away from him. This is my way of practicing what I preach. I just placed him carefully in the oven of college, ensured that the oven was good to go, and I'm now sitting back and enjoying the baking process. I know that he will call me if he needs me. I won't be watching the baking process for the most part, as I truly believe in the ingredients. I believe whether it's in work, play, relationships, or any other activity, *the only time that you lack trust in the process is when you lack faith in the ingredients.*

The baking process is an opportunity to change your surroundings. Time to take a break from the kitchen. Positive things come from changing where you stand. During the writing of this book, there were times that pages would flow out of me effortlessly. On others, I would find myself struggling to find four words. I found myself stuck. Yes, you have heard of it. They call it writer's block. It's the point where you run up against a brick wall. You can do no more. When most of us are confronted by these walls, we often shut down or give up. Others, the truly creative ones, the ones that really have their sprinkles, know that the wall is simply there to lead you in a different direction. It's not an obstacle, but rather an opportunity to plot a new course; a new course that leads you to new experiences. Experiences that will ultimately enrich your life.

When confronted by the wall don't be afraid or frustrated. Embrace it and use it as a chance to reboot. As I said in the beginning, I'm in the midst of a major reboot. For some of us, the reboot may not be so major. Along the way, I have found that reboots can come in all different sizes, shapes, and durations. For example, leading up to this recent reboot of drastic proportion, I found myself at my wits' end about six months prior. So much so that I hooked up the Airstream and took myself away from it all. Now, most of you are probably saying, "I could never do that, I don't have the time." I'm here to tell you that you may not be able to afford *not* to go.

As you can probably tell, I'm the epitome of an optimist. I pride myself on being able to project that attitude every day to the universe. But, at that time, I felt that life was starting to get the best of me. That pessimistic voice on my shoulder that I was paying little attention to was starting to win. My optimistic attitude of norm was depleted. So I hitched up the trailer and again cleared the airwaves so I could sort things out. I solicited the assistance of one of the most positive people that I know, Tony Robbins. I went into the nearest bookstore and bought Tony's book *Awakening the Giant Within.* Yes, at that point, I felt like I needed to slay some dragons and restore my self of old. What better way to do it than to energize myself through the words of another. It was my version of drinking a natural energy drink. It was my version of installing a fresh battery. It was my way of walking away from the oven during the baking stage to gain a fresh perspective. Often life brings you to a crossroads. Often the crossroads are noisy places and it's hard to concentrate. It's okay to step away and eliminate the background noise. It's okay to step away from the oven and let things bake.

Mott-Ohs

My idea of multitasking is lying down, falling into a deep sleep, having an awesome dream, snoring, and waking up reenergized. That's my idea of multitasking!

Small speed bumps become insurmountable mountains in the sleep-deprived mind.

In order for you to have a productive tomorrow, it is essential for you to obtain the proper rest today.

When one person is carrying the entire load, it will always have adverse effects on a relationship.

The solution is to release each other from what's all consuming.

The only time that you lack trust in the process is when you lack faith in the ingredients.

CHAPTER 16

WANNA LICK THE BOWL OR THE SPOON?

The baking process is all about following the prescribed steps to ensure success. It's about following the road map and staying between the lines so you arrive at a certain location. Yes, there is a recipe that really should be followed. Just as we discussed in the "Mix It Up" chapter, life is about mixing things up a bit. I have always said, *it's not about doing what's expected of you, but rather what's least expected.* Life is an opportunity. Life should be seized like a brass ring every chance you get without departing from the recipe for success. Every step of the baking process should be savored and made into a joyful act. Life is like a blank canvas and you're the brush. It's up to you to determine what your work of art looks like.

The other day, I was down in San Diego, California, and sitting by a pool. No, it's not as enticing as it may sound. It was February, and although the weather was warm, Mother Nature was showing her presence by adding some drizzle into the mix. I was sitting under an umbrella to escape. Why would I be sitting out at the pool in the rain? One word: kids. I was watching my girlfriend's daughter Victoria. She was insistent on going swimming. Swimming in the rain? Crazy to an adult, but it makes perfect sense to a child. I ask you, who is more sane? I believe it's the child. After all, you're going to get wet! Why let some raindrops get in the way? Anyway, on with the story. While I was sitting there, huddled under the umbrella, I noticed this little boy standing in the Jacuzzi. He was looking straight at me, or so I thought, with his tongue out. At first I thought, "That little snot is sticking his tongue out at me!" Before I gave him a tongue lashing, I realized he was trying to catch raindrops on his tongue. I sat there for a minute watching him and then, a huge smile came upon my face. This was definitely one of those Mott-Oh moments. Oh, the wonder and resolve of a child! There is never a thought of "why I shouldn't do something" but rather, "Can you imagine the possibility; the possibility of catching a raindrop on your tongue?" How magical would that be? The brass ring would have just landed on the tip of my tongue. Tear-drops from heaven! I'm in! I sprang from my position under the umbrella and started walking around the pool area, head tilted to the sky, with my tongue sticking out. Good thing nobody saw me, as they would have called security! There's a man in the pool area walking feverishly around the pool with his tongue out, and there are children down there. Save the children!!! Little did they know, the children were saving me. God forbid I act like a kid again! So I ask you, when did we stop chasing raindrops while using our tongue as the catchall? Has our ability to imagine and create things out of thin air vanished? I think not. Is it because we have become more conservative and have eased into a prescribed set of adult rules that make life a bit boring? I think so.

The other day, I was lying on the bed. My girlfriend had just placed her daughter in the tub. I was intently listening to her play. She was playing with her little critters. I had a spontaneous thought to depart from the norm and to cast away the bow lines of excepted practice. So I sprang from the bed and yelled! "I'm coming in!" I threw my wallet, cell phone, and keys on the bed and I jumped in the tub with all my clothes on. :-) If you could have seen the expression on her face, it was priceless. First it was, what are you doing in my bathtub? Then it was a yell to Mom to proclaim that Chris had finally lost it! Andrea came in and immediately scolded me. She was upset over the mess that I was about to make getting out of the tub with my clothes soaking wet. She too had drifted into that boring adult rut for a second where everything is conservative and vanilla. I didn't take her scolding too seriously, as I have become quite proficient at decoding her nonverbal style of communication. Andrea has certain facial expressions that contradict whatever is coming out of her mouth. When she makes what I call the "cute mad face," I know that all is good in the world of Chris.

So I sat there soaking wet and began to play with Victoria. Within minutes, the fact that I was in the tub and that I was wearing all my clothes didn't matter. Victoria quickly shifted back into the land of Victoria and I had joined her in her quest to play with the critters. Sometimes, if you really wish to join what others are doing, you must be willing to meet them on their level. In this case, the level was all about fun, and I rarely have trouble achieving that in life. Time passed on by and it was time to return to the land of the dry adults. I simply raised up, dried myself off, and threw my clothes in the dryer. No harm, no foul.

You must know that there was a grander plan in my head than just jumping in the tub. It wasn't simply an excuse for getting clean and doing my laundry all in one. It wasn't all about doing something that people did not expect me to do. It was about making memories. After having three kids myself, I've figured out that it's not necessarily the big things that you do, but rather the things that you do that make an impact. Three weeks had passed since my tub-diving incident, and all three of us were lying on the bed telling stories. Victoria all of a sudden lit up and she said with a giggle, "Chris, remember when you jumped in the tub with all your clothes on?" I looked over at Andrea and uttered these words: "mission accomplished!" My mission was to make a memory, and her recollection of the event proved that I not only made an impact but it was something that she would never forget. To this day, she now locks to the door to the bathroom. LOL—*not!* Although I will say this: as time has passed, Victoria, just like all of my own children, has started to grow from a little girl into a young lady. The days of her prancing around the house completely naked are over. The days of me being able to jump into the tub with her are long gone. Life moves so fast. An opportunity that exists today may not be there tomorrow. I encourage you to seize every opportunity, especially when it makes a lasting impression and/or a fond memory.

So my question to you is this: Would you like to lick the bowl or the spoon? Sometimes during the process, the real prize is not the end result, but the gifts that appear along the way. There was nothing better than licking the bowl or the spoon as a child. Now, as adults, we often just throw both in the sink. Life is not to be wasted. Life is full of priceless memories to lick up along the way. *Stop, drop, and taste life at every chance.*

Mott-Ohs

In life, it's not about doing what's expected of you, but rather what's least expected.

Stop, drop, and taste life at every chance.

CHAPTER 17

IS SOMETHING BURNING?

Have you ever been so busy that life started burning down around you? So much so that you couldn't even see or smell the smoke? Yes, suddenly you realize that your feet are on fire! You scurry for help only to find that the inferno is out of control! Many of us find ourselves in similar situations. Half of our mistakes originate from the fact that we aren't keeping a watchful eye on the kitchen. We're simply so tired, distracted, or consumed with items of measure that we take our eye off the ball. Funny thing is, the cupcakes were burning well before we could smell the smoke. Therefore, *it's essential to spot the signs of fire before the flames gets out of control in the kitchen.*

Despite our best efforts, there will always be fires, and they occur for a reason. Take, for instance, actual wildfires. We made every effort to reduce the number of wildfires for years. Thousands of dollars and countless hours of work were expended to reduce the destruction. While successful at first, we soon realized that we were doing more damage than good. In the wild, the act of fire promotes growth. The removal of overgrown plant life and/or clutter in the forests makes way for new species and life to emerge. Where there was once darkness there is now light, which is one of the main ingredients in every growth process on the planet. Where in your life has clutter overtaken the floor of your forest? Has it taken over to the extent that it's hard to move around or navigate? Is self-inflicted darkness inhibiting growth from happening in your life? Maybe it's time to set some intentional fires. Maybe it's time to clear away the forest canopy so that light can shine through. I'm not suggesting you set out-of-control fires, but possibly some controlled burns. *Sometimes it's essential to light a fire under your or someone else's butt to promote growth in certain areas.* Sometimes it's essential to clear the forest to promote growth that germinates and springs into new ideas and experiences.

We have learned over time that certain species of pines, known as fire climax pines, reproduce only during the event of extreme heat. When the wildfire occurs, the immense heat causes the pinecones to release millions and millions of seeds that have been just sitting and waiting. Once this happens, they fall to the ground as ambassadors of growth; they germinate and then spring to life as seedlings. Without this act of destruction, pine forests would cease to exist. So in life, when we have our own wildfires, something always emerges out of the ashes. Out of the burnt carnage comes something very special: an opportunity for growth. Just imagine if you could do it all over. If you could do it all over with the knowledge that you gained the first time, I bet the second go-round would be much more productive.

The question truly is, where do you climax in life and why are you holding back? During the growth cycles, we tend to learn the most. We learn the most while stretching our boundaries and, in many instances, when we make mistakes. Often we need to burn several batches of cupcakes to learn the perfect formula for baking. These burnt cupcakes serve as life's lessons. Mistakes in the real world are equivalent to nature's wildfires. Once we learn from these mistakes, we carry with us what I like to call *"the Golden Cupcake." These are the trophies achieved from learning life's lessons.*

Are you in the midst of a wildfire? Or are you standing in the aftermath? Either way, how have you chosen to look at it? Starting over is not a bad thing. It's an opportunity to reboot. Seize the opportunity to go in any direction. As sixteen million people sit unemployed in America, most of them lie dormant just like the pine seed. They are waiting for an opportunity to be released and to spring into action. Many sit waiting for the phone to ring. But *the wise ones recognize the crossroads for what they really are: an opportunity to reinvent.*

Was I a victim of the economic downturn, or was I just given the greatest opportunity? Often we get locked into a certain direction in life. Now is the time to bust out. Now is the time to do something amazing. Think about it. Being unemployed is obviously one of scariest and most stressful events that a person may endure. On one hand, you don't have the stress of working, but on the other hand, you have the stress of not working. You have just traded one for the other, and, depending on your financial situation, one might argue as to which is worse. It ranks right up there on the list of life's most stressful events. These are as follows, and not in any particular order:

Death of a spouse
Divorce
Marital separation
Jail term or death of a family member
Personal injury or illness
Marriage
Change in financial status
Marital reconciliation or retirement
Pregnancy
Loss of job due to termination

Think about the list a bit. These top ten stressors often come all at the same time. They are not just flying solo. For instance, loss of a job due to termination is most often sure to affect your financial status. If it then leads to a divorce or a strain on your relationship, you have just swallowed three of the top ten list in one gulp. I personally have swallowed more than one at a time. Shortly after my mom passed away, I renovated my house, got a divorce, changed my financial situation, and started a new job. That, my friends, is one big cup of stress. Any way you spell it, it still sounds the same: no fun.

When it comes to losing your job, I'm in no way trying to trivialize the event. However, as much as it's stressful, it can also be exciting. Throughout this book, I talk about how *life is a series of perceptions. Perceptions form our reality.* For those of you that are currently unemployed, you will find that the event just gets more stressful from inaction. If you wait in indecision, it can lead to a compound negative effect. Just as you choose to wallow in your misery of being unemployed, you too can make the conscious decision to cause change. Think about it. We spend most of our lives employed and searching for extra time in the day. Time is a valuable commodity. Once you become unemployed, time is still the commodity that it once was, yet no longer is it scarce. Time instantly shifts on your side. Why not put that time to work and seize the opportunity to reinvent yourself? I guarantee if you choose to put one foot in front of another and choose action rather than inaction, you will automatically open doors that you didn't even know or believe were there.

I, like most of you, have fallen down and gotten back up. In school we are taught that if you fall off the swing, you should dust yourself off and try again. Adults forget this life lesson. We become paralyzed by fear; the fear of making mistakes. This is indeed the worst mistake that we can make. *It's imperative that we induce self-imposed, selective amnesia when it comes to our past mistakes.* Learn the lesson, but don't let the memory of the mistake deter your future efforts.

For those football fans out there, you have probably heard sportscasters say that a short-term memory is a key ingredient in a successful quarterback. In many games, the quarterback will turn the ball over to the other team by throwing an interception. The quarterback then returns to the bench and is forced to think about and analyze the unsuccessful play. If he dwells on this mistake, when he is given the opportunity to play again, he will often not live up to his potential. If he learns from his mistakes and has selective amnesia, he is more apt to move his team forward in the game and be successful.

My son Jordan was the quarterback of his high school football team. Yes, he was an athlete, but never was he a natural-born athlete. In fact, when he was playing Pop Warner football, one of his coaches questioned his mom and me about whether we were forcing Jordan to play. He asked us this question because Jordan physically did not display that killer instinct. He was timid, to say the least, but what he lacked in toughness and aggression, he made up for in heart, passion, and the desire to play the game. As a result of his continuous drive and dedication, he eventually turned himself into a six-foot rock and secured a position as the quarterback of the Santa Clara Bruins. Jordan would tend to throw just as many interceptions as he would completions.

What I admired about him was his ability to get upset, shake it off, and then rebound immediately by doing something positive.

There are two kinds of mistakes in life: those that teach you a lesson and those that should have taught you a lesson. If you are paralyzed by fear or let your mistakes be an impediment to springing into action, you are most certainly destined to repeat them. Someone once told me, *"Only a fool steps in the same pile of dog poop twice."* To this day, I have never forgotten that expression. It's imperative that we embrace our mistakes, handle them with grace, and use them as stepping stones to cross the rockiest of terrain along this path we call life.

I admit, I have been stubborn when it comes to accepting life's lessons. There are those who choose to step in the same pile of dog poop twice just to get a good look at where not to step. Then there are those that step in it twice because they refuse to admit that they have stepped in it in the first place. True humility and accountability are lacking in America. The political arena these days is a prime example of this. Each party is constantly pointing fingers at the other instead of doing worthwhile work and the heavy lifting required. In fact, the only accountability and humility that I ever see from politicians is when they are exposed or forced into confession. *Humility and confession should never be the fallback position.* Every couple of months it seems as though there's another political or moral scandal. Someone has cheated on either his or her spouse or constituents by a breach of ethics. It's only until the cheater is caught red handed that he or she retreats and apologizes. We, as human beings, are born imperfect. When we stop believing this and start to think that we know it all, this is when we tend to dive into life's black holes and are susceptible to betraying or compromising our moral compass.

I believe that the good times of the last decade or so have created a sense of complacency and entitlement. We often tell ourselves that we deserve and are entitled to certain things. Admit it. You have said these words. "I deserve that promotion." "I should be getting a raise." "I should be given more responsibility." "I should be able to afford all the luxuries of the highly successful." Good times and a lack of appreciation have created a society of entitlement.

As our economy has taken a downward spiral and now sits idle in what many say is equal to a depression, we are just now starting to see a shift in this sense of entitlement. It has now changed to a sense of urgency and a sense of gratitude. When you take something away that people would normally take for granted, you automatically create scarcity. *Through scarcity comes appreciation and a renewed sense of worth.* When jobs in America were plentiful, workers would discard them like trash. They would use the one they had to leverage their position to get another. As the supply and demand tables turn and jobs have now become scarce, they in turn have become more sought after and valued. The days of "I'm entitled to that raise or promotion" have been quickly replaced by "I'm so fortunate to have my job" and "How can I do more to keep this job?"

Ten years ago, I was probably at the lowest point in my life. My mother had fallen ill and was diagnosed with pancreatic cancer. After being diagnosed in November, she passed in February. At the time, I had ripped down my house to one wall and had moved my entire family into a motor home in the front yard. Now picture this. My mom had just died, there is one working toilet (kind of), and my wife at the time, the three kids, two cats, a dog, and a bird were living in a three-hundred-square-foot motor home in the driveway. Needless to say, the marriage, under the stress and strain of the situation, failed. I had hit rock bottom, or so I thought.

I remember the day that I walked into my newly remodeled three-thousand-square-foot house. Half of the furniture had just been removed due to the divorce, and I was alone. All alone! The kids had left for their mom's, and for the first time in twelve years, the house was dead silent. Not a good silence; in fact, a silence that pierced my heart. As I stood there, in my empty living room, I dropped to my knees and sobbed. Mom was gone. The silence that came with the absence of children was unnerving. My marriage was over. What did I do to deserve this? Why me? I immediately left the house and went to Home Depot just to avoid the silence.

As I look back at that moment, I now realize that when I decided to run away from my problem, I was doing myself a disservice. What? Home Depot was running away? Yes, in a sense it was. I was saying, I'm not ready to deal with this and I think I can mask my feelings by creating some short-term fix. Admit it. We all have our vices. For some, it's food. For some, it's new shoes. For others, it might be smoking or some kind of drug. In my case, it was spending, and along with it I threw in alcohol abuse just for fun. I use the term "abuse" as I truly believe that most things are okay in moderation. However, when you use things to escape or to mask your true feelings, you are abusing the substance and, more importantly, yourself.

As I walked into Home Depot to escape, I felt that I could regain control of my happiness by spending and that I could silence my sorrow. Little did I know that I was just replacing one bad situation with another. From that point forward and for a good couple of years, I was a drunk and what I like to call a spendaholic. I had made the fatal mistake of choosing to become a victim. I chose to waste my life in the bottom of a tequila bottle and to surround myself with shiny, materialistic possessions, only to mask and numb my feelings.

By night, I was a drunk and by day, a walking disaster. I would search out people to talk to, only to drag them into my misery. Picture this: Imagine if all of your mistakes were burnt cupcakes, and suddenly you strung them into a necklace and hung them around your neck. Then take the mistakes (burnt cupcakes) of those around you and hang those around your neck as well. That was Chris Mott. I was "that guy." All my problems and even those of others were front and center. Too bad that people couldn't really see the burnt cupcakes. If they could, they would have the chance to save themselves. At this point, I feel the need to issue a public apology for my behavior and wish to thank you all for your support and patience with me.

Have you ever heard the expression *"It's not the baggage that's the problem…it's how you carry it"*? I was the poster child for how not to carry your baggage. I was drinking by night and consumed with rehashing every one of my burnt cupcakes by day. Anyone within a five-foot radius was cheap therapy. Why? Because I made the choice that I was not going to learn from my mistakes. I made the choice that I was going to wallow in self-pity. Seriously, my mother had to be turning over in her urn. If she had been alive she would have given me a swift kick in the rear and told me to get over it!

For the first time in my life, I had become "the victim." Stripped of my self-motivation, I was a ship without an anchor, clearly off course, and just drifting through life. The problem was, for the first time in my life, I had failed to take accountability. You see in life, everyone is accountable. Nobody is innocent. There is always room for improvement. *A failure to recognize your own accountability serves up a destiny that much resembles the footsteps of the past.*

While drifting at sea with all my burnt cupcakes, relationships came and relationships went. I had built this fortress around my heart to keep everyone at a safe distance. Again, I chose to be paralyzed by the mistakes of the past. To all the women that I dated during this period, I'm sorry. I was fun to be around. I was spending money like it grew on trees, and I was a happy drunk. But, as my girlfriends were honestly opening up and giving themselves to me, I was hiding behind a wall of pain. How could I be hurt again if I didn't expose myself? So I took my heart and locked it away in a safe place. What a disservice to those around me. What a disservice to myself. Again, I apologize.

Let's take this opportunity to take a sidebar. As I have said, part of making mistakes is learning from them. Just as important is apologizing for them. When I say apologizing, I mean sincerely apologizing. Not only to the person you hurt, wronged, or misled, but to yourself. We don't really put the burnt cupcakes away and learn from them unless we sincerely make amends and let them go. *Nothing is better at diffusing a difficult situation than a sincere apology.* Learn how to sincerely apologize and then ask how you can make the situation right. Sincerity is the key to this equation. Everything is better in life when it's sincere. Someone once said, "If you want to get in the last word, start with a sincere apology."

Back to my story of wallowing in self-pity, lacking accountability, not giving life 100 percent, and failing to apologize to myself for the mistakes in my past. Just as I mentioned in a previous chapter, you need to learn how to let things go. Too many people carry their mistakes with them and beat themselves up for way too long. Often they fail to recognize that a mistake is a stepping stone rather than the end of the road. *Why be defined by yesterday's actions today?*

Those who use the mistakes as stepping stones realize that a batch of burnt cupcakes is merely an excuse to make a better batch. Life often has a divine plan and it sends you back to see, feel, and experience the process again. Think about it: even the best baseball players strike out most of the time. A good batting average is .300. That means a batter is getting on base only three out of every ten at-bats. Baseball players know that life, and more so success, is all about the number of at-bats. Every time you step up to the plate, you have a clean slate in front of you. Every time you step up to the plate, you have the potential to hit a home run. Every repetition gives you an experience that leads to expertise. *Through repetition comes excellence. With excellence comes freedom. With freedom comes the ultimate form of creativity. Those failing to take risks, those caught in their own self-made paralysis, are those who seem to creep through life at a snail's pace.*

Steady as she goes. It's like coming up behind a car on a one-lane road. The speed limit is clearly sixty miles per hour. The car in front of you is going forty-five. What do you do? Do you play it safe and just follow at forty-five miles per hour in the hopes that the driver will eventually turn off, or do you take a risk? Do you take the calculated risk and pass him or her? Most often the calculated risk will get you to your goal much sooner.

In this instance, the goal for me was to get over a very turbulent time in my life. It was to move past the hurt of a difficult divorce and the agony of losing my mother. I chose to stay behind the car on the two-lane highway. I made no aggressive moves to move myself forward or past the situation. In fact, I was my worst enemy as I made the unconscious decision to do everything that would slow down my road to recovery.

Yes, my kitchen was clearly burning, but I did nothing to put out the fire. In many cases I fueled the fire. How is the state of your kitchen? Is it on fire or is it about to burst into flames? Are you prepared to deal with the issues and use them as an opportunity to grow?

Often at work, we are professional firefighters, but when it comes to the home front, we choose to look in the other direction. We are quick to offer advice, but very stubborn when it comes to taking it ourselves. Are you a procrastinator?

Do you purposely put things off today to deal with them tomorrow? Have you ever noticed that a small flame today is most likely to be a full blaze by tomorrow? We need to recognize the potential hot spots in life and deal with them in a time-sensitive manner. We must extinguish them before they do real irreparable damage.

So the turning point was the day that I took control again. It was about two or three years after my divorce. I had maxed out all of my credit cards, and had built my entire lifestyle around partying and drinking twenty-four/seven. I had designed a style of communication with my ex-wife that was all about controlling the method in which we would interact. Now that I look back, what I had devised was the most absurd method of interaction possible. I didn't want anything to do with my ex-wife. So I did everything that I could to limit my contact with her. All of our correspondence was by way of e-mail. To make the kid exchange, we would meet in a neutral location, the cars would pull up alongside each other, the kids would jump out and switch cars, and all without a word. It was like a late-night drug exchange, and I was the author of the plan. What was I teaching my kids? Well, let's just say it wasn't anything good. Yes, I had taken control of the communication and interaction. I rationalized that it was all for my own self-preservation. How selfish was that? It was a selfish attempt to repair my beaten-down ego. Ego is defined as an inflated opinion of self, an exaggerated sense of self-importance, and a feeling of superiority to other people. *Those that get caught up in their sense of self-importance, their egos, find it hard to forgive.* Looking back, it was super selfish, and to my kids, whom I absolutely adore, please accept my sincere apology.

Never would we talk on the phone. Now, does that sound like a guy that was taking control? Does it sound like a guy that was facing his problems, or does that sound like a guy that was running from them? Yes, I was running away from my problems and at full speed! Now that I look back, it was so stupid. It seems so obvious now that the dust has settled. Hindsight is definitely 20/20 vision.

I was extremely protective of my kids while I was going through the process. At every turn, I wanted to shelter them from my agony. However, what

I wasn't saying in words, I was communicating through my actions. Never would I say a harsh word about their mother, but by not communicating with her, I was speaking volumes. It was, to say the least, a terrible lesson, and if I could take it back, I would in a heartbeat. Just as I'm telling you to take your burnt cupcakes and place them aside, I too have done the same. I have chalked this up as a major life lesson, apologized to my kids, and I now let this serve as a teaching tool to move forward and help others in life.

Eventually, I decided to change my situation. I decided to pull myself out of the well of self-pity and live again. I decided to call my ex-wife on the phone and talk to her. To this day, I remember her reaction. The sound of utter disbelief in her voice was priceless. She was mystified that I was on the phone. Of course, I just acted like it was no big deal. That day was my turning point. Instead of walking through life in a negative, powerless fashion, I took a step in a positive direction and truly regained the control in my life. I had wasted two years of my life running away or masking my true feelings, but I was done.

Sometimes in life it takes something to shock us out of the rut. It could be an event, something that someone says, or something as trivial as a fortune cookie. Yes, a fortune cookie. I was finishing up Chinese takeout one night, and as I opened up a fortune cookie, it hit me. Sometimes the signs in life are subtle. On other occasions, they come in written form. My fortune on that given night might as well have said, "Chris, it's time to take control again." As fortune cookies sometimes do, it was more geared to the masses than calling me by my first name. It simply stated, *"You are the master of every situation."* Time came to an absolute standstill. The fortune hit me like a ton of bricks. There might as well have been angels singing in the background and a bright light shining from above. Yes, I had an epiphany. Just so we are clear, an epiphany is the sudden realization or comprehension of the larger essence or meaning of something. At that moment, I realized that I had drifted away from what I believed to be one of my core philosophies in life: the philosophy that you can make or break any situation by how you view and react to it. It was like someone jump-started my engine and I was back on track. Someone was saying to me, "Chris, *you have more control and power through positive action than through negative actions."* Often it's difficult in life to face our troubles head on. I'm here to tell you from experience that the head-on approach will land you miles ahead in the long run. Running from our fears and holding ourselves hostage to the events of the past only serves to shift the control into the hands of others. So from that day on, I decided that I would never allow myself to forget that principle. This was truly the day that I regained my sprinkles!

Mott-Ohs

It's essential to spot the signs of fire before the flames get out of control in the kitchen.

Sometimes it's essential to light a fire under your or someone else's butt to promote growth in certain areas.

"The Golden Cupcakes" are the trophies achieved from learning life's lessons.

The wise ones recognize the crossroads for what they really are: an opportunity to reinvent.

Life is a series of perceptions. Perceptions form our reality.

It's imperative that we induce self-imposed, selective amnesia when it comes to our past mistakes.

It's difficult to dampen the spirit with feathers to protect you.

There are two kinds of mistakes in life: those that teach you a lesson and those that should have taught you a lesson.

Only a fool steps in the same pile of dog poop twice.

Humility and confession should never be the fallback position.

"Through scarcity comes appreciation and a renewed sense of self worth."

"It's not the baggage that's the problem...it's how you carry it."

A failure to recognize your own accountability serves up a destiny that much resembles the past.

Nothing is better at diffusing a difficult situation than a sincere apology.

Why be defined by yesterday's actions today?

Through repetition comes excellence. With excellence comes freedom. With freedom comes the ultimate form of creativity.

Those failing to take risks, those caught in their own self-made paralysis, are those who seem to creep through life at a snail's pace.

Those that get caught up in their sense of self-importance, their egos, find it hard to forgive.

You are the master of every situation.

You have more control and power through positive action than through negative actions.

CHAPTER 18

AN ALTERNATE BATCH

A t this very minute, America is sitting at a full stop. We are sitting at a railroad crossing. The gates have come down, the lights are flashing red, and a slow-moving, never-ending stretch of train cars called the recession is moving down the tracks. Much as if a train had derailed, traffic has come to an earth-shattering halt and everyone is standing, waiting, for that green light to get us moving again.

So my question to you is simply this: How often does life try to derail you? How often does life come to a grinding halt due to some unforeseen circumstance? I bet the answer is often. I believe this probably happens every day to some degree. So the true question is, if we have grown accustomed to life's roadblocks, why are we not doing anything about them? Why weren't we better prepared for this recession? My answer to this question is that Americans have become one-dimensional.

Let's face it. As we grow older, we often get locked into grooves, such as careers, investments strategies, spending habits, family patterns, and other lifestyle choices. Sometimes these grooves are healthy, and other times they are unhealthy. We tend to gravitate towards things we know or areas that have proven to be comfortable in our lifetime. These grooves sometimes become ruts and serve as blockades when it comes to reaching the level of satisfaction that we desire.

As these patterns in life appear, we tend to fall towards them as safety nets. It makes sense unless the safety net is being held up by only one rope. When your one lifeline is cut for whatever the reason, you're screwed. You fall and fall hard. You often find yourself wounded in many ways. Depending on the situation, the wounds might be financial, emotional, or even physical. Once wounded, the journey back to stable ground seems even harder, and in many cases the climb is slower and prolonged.

As you lie there licking your wounds or dusting yourself off, you often find yourself wishing that you had packed a parachute. If only I had prepared for this! If you burn a batch of cupcakes or there is a random derailment during the baking process, do you have a backup plan?

Consider the last question. I specifically mention two causes leading up to a derailment. One is you and the other is a random event. I sincerely believe that *there are only two types of derailments in life: those that are just thrown into the mix and those that you throw into the mix yourself.* You must identify their origin so you can spot them. If they are self-inflicted derailments, you can take preventive steps to ensure that they don't happen in the first place. Just as we explained, issues are like failing asphalt with foundation problems, and the same holds true for derailments. You must recognize the underlying threat so you can focus on prevention. You must find the cracks and fix the foundation problems before attempting to put your train back on the track. If you fail at this, your train is sure to derail again.

So what really is an alternate batch in life? Simply put, it's a plan B. When I was attending college, I would occasionally come across students that were pursuing a major and a minor in two fields of study. I quickly dismissed them as crazy, overzealous individuals with the need to prove something. Now older and wiser, I ask everyone, *"Do you have a major and minor in life?"* After all, we all know that life can throw you a curveball at times. *Those that are ready and prepared to handle life's curveballs are less apt to strike out.* Being ambidextrous in every facet of life just gives you a fallback plan, a safety net. Without this fallback plan, you tend to fall harder, as there's nothing but air between you and the ground.

The key ingredient to having a plan B is simply being prepared. I had to write this chapter twice. When I initially wrote it, I was speaking from mostly a position of speculation. However, after I wrote it, life threw one of those inevitable curveballs my way. For the first time in almost thirty years, I was facing the unemployment line. Yes, thirty years. I had secured a job at age thirteen. From that point on, there was never a time that I didn't either have a job, two jobs, or was searching for the next opportunity. I speak from experience when I say never put all your eggs in one basket. I speak with authority when I say *never let your fate rest in the hands of others when they are clearly only looking out for themselves.* Now, that's a harsh statement coming from a person who some people like to call "Little Miss Mary Sunshine." I suppose I've been given that title since I tend to look at life through rose-colored glasses. I tend to err on the side of finding the good in others and the world. I'm definitely a glass-half-full guy. However, there are certain realities in life, and as much as I like to focus on the good, I know that the bad exists. At many a turn in life, there are people, things, and circumstances that are ready and willing to trip you up. We have to be prepared to deal with these situations. Does it mean that we walk through life on eggshells waiting for something bad to happen? Does it mean that we sleep with one eye open? Does it mean that we walk through life being afraid of our own shadow? No, but it does mean that we become prepared for all situations and have a plan B poised and waiting in the wings. *Foresight owes its 20/20 vision to hindsight. Those that are ready for the rebound are the quickest to score again in life.*

These grooves or ruts that we ease into leave us few options. They promote the one-dimensional lifestyle that I mentioned previously. To be poised with a plan B, you must develop ways to diversify in certain sectors of your life. As a result of diversification, we become protected from one catastrophic setback in life. Think of it this way: If I have four trains all in the same general area, they are probably all encountering the same weather. If extreme weather hits, the likelihood of all my trains being adversely affected is good. However, if I have trains in four different geographic areas, the chances of them all being affected is slim. This is called diversifying your assets. Let's drill down a bit deeper as to where you might choose to diversify.

Finances

The recent stock market crash is proof that *having all of your eggs in one basket is never a smart strategy.* Millions of people had little control over their retirement dollars disappearing. They were not actively managing their investments. The best and the brightest financial consultants preached investing in 401(k) plans. In some cases, this is a good strategy. Compounding savings, company matching, pretax advantage, and earning interest through an established and routine investment plan are very wise moves. It's also another example of how diversification can save your financial life. Take, for instance, if you were to have all your savings invested in some risky start-up. Imagine the market taking a nosedive or some external force rendering the start-up's product obsolete. You would lose your shirt. In other words, you would not only lose your eggs, but the basket as well. *When it comes to investing, sticking all your bets on one racehorse puts you one twisted ankle from financial disaster.* On the other hand, if you have some dollars invested in oil, some in real estate, some in high tech, some in gold, it is less likely that one oil spill or one twisted ankle is going to affect all of your assets. You may tank on one of them, but the others will carry you through.

As I mentioned before, *most people get into trouble in life when they are not active.* In this case, I am referring to active versus inactive investing. The majority of investors today will make their initial 401(k) allocations when they start a new job and never touch them again. It's like putting your entire family on a boat and then pushing them out to sea. When you're not on the boat, there is nothing to guide them or ensure that they are heading in the right direction. It's essential to be able to make course changes along the way if you notice certain trends that are keeping you from reaching your destination. When we make these course corrections, we become semiactive investors. Why semiactive? Because when it comes to the stock market, you can only ever be semiactive. Yes, you can do your research as to the stability of a company, but you will never be in full control with others running the show. You are at the mercy of how the principals choose to run the company.

A more active investment vehicle would be real estate. Owning real estate is an extremely active way to invest. You control every aspect except for the strength of the market. You choose the location and type of asset to buy. You decide which resident or which tenant to place in the piece of real estate. You dictate how well the asset is maintained and what kind of amenities it has compared to its competition. In turn, you control the amount of income that you derive from the asset. Due to just some of these reasons, real estate, over the long haul, is a very safe and at most times very lucrative investment.

One of the main ideas that we have been discussing is scarcity. Through scarcity, things become more valuable. If you are choosing to buy a one-of-a-kind property, you are investing in something sought after. Land is limited in nature. There is only so much land on the planet, and the population continues to grow at an alarming rate. When applying the simple principles of supply and demand, it stands to reason that if land mass isn't growing, but the population is, the demand for real estate will forever increase.

Health and Fitness

As I've mentioned throughout the book, I recently became a long-distance runner. The more that I ran at the age of forty-two, the more that I found my body breaking down. Training for marathons is tough work, and there is a ton of time invested in hitting the trails to log running hours. The more that the body endures the continuous pounding of running, the more prone it is to injury. In my case, it was my knees. So what did I do? I went to plan B. I always loved to bike. So I started mixing some biking into my daily or weekly exercise regimen. Then I added some swimming, and again the diversification paid off.

When you just focus on one type of exercise, you tend to get into a rut when it comes to results. After all, you are repeating the same exercise over and over. Therefore, it has the same results on the muscle groups involved. At certain points, your results start to plateau. Your muscle groups become accustomed to the repetition of the exercise. That's why many physical trainers talk about muscle confusion. It's essential in training to mix up exercises and to purposely disrupt routines to reach greater fitness success. Muscle confusion is a physical trainer's plan B. Think about it. When have you hit a plateau in life?

Was it because you were doing the same thing over and over yet expecting different results? Just like in the baking process, it's smart to mix it up a bit.

Friendship

I may have over two thousand Facebook friends, but when it comes to real friends, friends that I can truly count on, I probably can count them all on my two hands. After all, if I chose to invest my time in keeping up with and supporting all of my Facebook friends, I wouldn't be a very good friend to anyone. You can only do so much, and when it comes to friends, it's wise to diversify in a picky fashion. It's essential to invest in friendships that will augment your life. I often watch those television reality shows that track the lives of certain people. You know, *The Housewives of Train Wreck County.* Can you imagine if your friendship network was like that in real life? The entire world would be on sedatives. With friends like that, who needs friends?

I was sitting at a graduation luncheon for my oldest son last summer. I could tell that even though he was happy in achieving this milestone, he was sad to be leaving the friendships that he had made during his high school years. I asked him to speculate which friendships he thought would stand the test of time. As he named about six names, I quickly pointed to certain individuals sitting around the table. These were the friends that had passed the test of time in my life. There were friends from high school and college. It was proof to my son that true friendships endure. We make friendships at all stages of our lives. Some come and some go. Those that stick, the core group, need to be cherished.

Each friend has his or her own place. My daughter Kaley wrote on her Face-book page. "Every day is a learning experience, the people who hurt you don't matter, the people who walk out aren't worth chasing, and *all the people that belong in your life will work to make sure they are where they are supposed to be.*" I highlight that last sentence because this truly is the essence of my mes-sage. The secret is about having the right mixture and the right ingredients. I believe that the friends with whom we choose to surround ourselves are there for a reason. Knowing their roles and their purpose for being there is extremely helpful. *True friends will prop you up when you need support, make you laugh when you need a giggle, and will just be there when something seems to be missing.* True friends will tell you what you need to hear, not what you want to hear. Oscar Wilde once said, "A true friend stabs you in the front."

Love

Love needs to come from everywhere. No, I am not suggesting that you should have ten girlfriends, boyfriends, spouses, or love interests, but rather a love network. Love truly comes in all different forms. You can receive love from friendship. You can receive another type from family. There is the love from a spouse. They're all unique in their own way and enrich our lives. Those of us without love in our lives will often feel like something is missing.

Love, like friendship, needs to be nurtured. Without water, the garden ceases to grow. If one plant receives all the nutrients, then the plants around it are sure to die and cease to exist. We all have met with new love in our life. Sometimes it's so overwhelming that we tend to push away or take for granted the love coming from other places. It may be intentional or unintentional. However, the end result is the same. The love network is compromised as a love monopoly occurs. Monopolies are prohibited because they create unhealthy situations. *Does a love monopoly exist in your life?* If so, you need to correct it and quick. The best thing about love is there's an infinite supply. It's up to you how you diversify.

Work

Are you punching the clock just so you can hear the whistle blow at the end of the day? Are you simply doing your time so you can collect a paycheck? Maybe you're one of the millions of Americans that's fallen into a career rut. Are you doing what you want to do or rather what you feel you must? Day after day it's the same old grind. Have you ever heard the expression "Another day, another dollar?" This is where a one-dimensional routine is born. *Monotony is born out of routine.* Being one-dimensional in your professional life is a death sentence waiting to be carried out. In these changing times, you need to be able to change like the wind. You need to learn not only your job, but the job of everyone around you. This is being what I call a double-threat guy.

A double-threat guy is one who can handle multiple situations, skills, and tasks. The double threat is way more valuable than someone who is perceived as one-dimensional.

Are you working to live or do you live to work? There can't be one reason. You must identify all the reasons and motivations. Your overall happiness depends on it. Perhaps you are pursuing a passion, but if that's not the case, maybe you are supporting a family that you love. Perhaps you are pursuing a lifelong goal or expanding your horizons and enhancing your sense of balance in life. *No matter what the reason, the more positive motivation that you have for working, the more fulfilled you will be.*

Rest and Play

I was thinking about how active my father is these days. He's eighty and has slowed down considerably. He is the walking definition of falling into a rut and doing nothing to work his way out. He's decided to adopt a very sedentary lifestyle. Then I compared his level of activity to other eighty-year-olds that I know. Just as in life, everyone has his or her own energy level, and everyone chooses his or her own path.

I think it's a travesty. Often when we retire and have the time to pursue enjoyable activities, our energy level downshifts. We spend much of our time yearning for more time and wishing we could expand our horizons. Then, when we get older and our physical ability starts to limit us, we tend to fall into that trap of believing what our body is saying. We buy into the idea that because of our advanced age or our declining energy levels, we cannot embrace life with the same vigor. Desire and that can-do attitude are not exclusive to just the young. Your body may change over the years, but your mind can eternally sip from the fountain of youth if you so choose. It's your mind that dictates the radius of your life.

You must diversify your interests and mix things up a bit. Just as my father has decided to sink into a permanent state of down time, you need to *ensure that too much of a good thing doesn't become bad.* You must steer away from a one-dimensional lifestyle. Diversity leads to balance, and balance leads to strength in life. You must have an alternate batch standing ready.

Mott-Ohs

There are only two types of derailments in life: those that are just thrown into the mix and those that you throw into the mix.

Do you have a major and minor in life?

Those that are ready and prepared to handle life's curveballs are less apt to strike out in life.

Never let your fate rest in the hands of others when they are clearly only looking out for themselves.

Foresight owes its 20/20 vision to hindsight.

Those that are ready for the rebound are the quickest to score again in life.

Having all of your savings in one place is never a smart strategy.

When it comes to investing, sticking all your bets on one racehorse puts you one twisted ankle from financial disaster.

Most people get into trouble in life when they are not active.

All the people who belong in your life will work to make sure they are where they are supposed to be.

True friends will prop you up when you need support, make you laugh when you need a giggle, and will just be there when something seems to be missing.

Love, like friendship, needs to be nurtured. Without water the garden ceases to grow.

Does a love monopoly exist in your life?

Monotony is born out of routine.

No matter what the reason, the more positive motivation that you have for working, the more fulfilled you will be.

Ensure that too much of a good thing doesn't become a bad thing.

CHAPTER 19

TIMER'S ABOUT TO GO OFF

L*ife is all about timing. It's all about being in the right place at the right time.* Everything that happens, whether it's a positive or negative event, is due to positioning. The question is, are you in position or out of position?

Think about it. Was it a promotion that you received, an account that you landed, a relationship that you started, or a contest that you won? Regardless of the circumstance, there were steps that you took to position yourself in the right place at the right time. It might not have been planned or a conscious decision, but either way, you positioned yourself for something positive to happen.

On the other side of the fence, was it that speeding ticket? Were you counseled at work? Maybe you lost your job. Maybe it was a relationship that went south. If you're honest, there were probably things that you did to contribute. Was it consciously driving above the speed limit? Maybe you were lacking effort in the workplace. Did you fail to give the relationship the attention that it deserved? We can't control everything in the universe, but we can steer things in certain directions based on our actions. *If you're standing there waiting for your stars to align, you might want to consider giving them a little nudge.*

Some consider life's happenings as fate, and maybe it is. I'm a staunch believer in the law of karma. What goes around comes around. However, the realist in me believes that it can't all be predetermined. I believe that you can stack the deck in your favor. It's like trying to become a doctor. It's a much harder task to achieve and downright impossible if you haven't finished or attended medical school. Just as there are directions to whip up the perfect batch of cupcakes, so too are there prescribed requirements for being a doctor. This rationale applies to any goal or achievement that you set for yourself. Crafting a plan and making the right choices when it comes to achieving these goals will increase your probability of realizing them.

Today, approximately sixteen million people are out of work. Ten million of those people aren't doing anything to posture themselves for success. Most of them are so caught up in their last position that they don't realize it's time to reposition. What do I mean by reposition? When you're out of work and looking towards the future, you have an opportunity to go in a totally new direction. Scary! Yes, to most people it is. The thought of change is foreign. Rather than viewing it in a negative way, we should choose to view it as an opportunity. All of us in America have fallen into the trap of entitlement. Things have been so good for so long that we feel as though we are entitled. We are not entitled to anything. *We inherit what we strive and work for in life.* Rather than the era of entitlement, this is now the era of reward based on positioning.

You've heard the expression, "I need to get my foot in the door." This is exactly what I am talking about. So many people are sitting at home and are nowhere near the front door. You must get out there and make things happen. Opportunities won't come looking for you. Rather, you need to drive yourself toward your desires. You have to position yourself where people will notice you. It's a game of numbers. It's like placing all your money on one horse. You could be waiting all day for a winner. However, if you put a little money on many horses, one of them is bound to win and you're off to the races.

Patience and timing go hand in hand. Knowing when to hold back and wait takes great practice. In other words, if you were to pull the cupcakes out of the oven before the proper amount of baking time, you would probably find that the cupcakes were underdone. They would lack the proper consistency and be too gooey to eat or decorate. I was never much of a country and western music fan, but one line from Kenny Rogers's song "The Gambler" comes to mind: "You've got to know when to hold 'em, know when to fold 'em." This song speaks volumes about having good timing in life. It's about making smart decisions to win the ultimate game. For the sake of this analogy, we are talking about the game of life. Sometimes you have to fold and lose the hand to end up winning all the chips in the end. It's all about timing in life, and even more so about appreciating that there's a time and place for everything. Patience is a virtue.

I have spent much time and energy evaluating the idea of appreciation these days. I was recently taking a walk with my girlfriend in the backwoods of Pennsylvania, and I asked her, "When do the tables turn? When do we truly start to appreciate things in life?" Now, you may be thinking that you are an appreciative person, but I am talking about true appreciation. True appreciation is when you recognize everything that goes on around you. You go out of your way to truly appreciate the greatness of what you have rather than dwelling on what you don't have.

I suppose my speculation was due to timing. I was walking around my childhood stomping grounds. I had walked this path a thousand times in my youth. On this visit, I seemed to notice different things and appreciate more. Allow me to give you a few examples. In my teens, I would have been screaming down this path on a four-wheeler or a dirt bike. If I wasn't screaming down the path, I was walking it with a shotgun in hand and thinking about what I could shoot or destroy. These days, I have replaced the four-wheeler with a pair of walking shoes, and I purposely travel the path a lot slower as not to miss anything. I have swapped the shotgun for a camera in one hand and the loving hand of my girlfriend in the other. I'm constantly aware of the touch of my girlfriend's warm hand in the palm of mine and the sights and sounds around me.

Occasionally, I stop and ask my girlfriend to listen. Possibly it's a bird chirping away in a tree or the creaking sound of hemlock trees swaying in the wind. Yes, in our youth we are flying down the road of life. We seem to only catch the highlights. At some age, or some point in life, this seems to shift. What's the cause of this shift? It seems as if it's caused by either timing or a life-altering event.

Suffering the loss of my mom shocked me into a state of appreciation. This was one of those times that life was force-feeding me a cup of perspective. *Life's cup of perspective is sure to shock you into a true state of appreciation every time.* Like a cold splash of water in the morning, these are the instances where we realize too late that we have been robbed of the opportunity to fully appreciate.

Do we really need to be shocked into a state of appreciation by a life-altering event? Must we wait until we reach a ripe old age to genuinely appreciate all that life has to offer? I say no. We need to understand that life is precious and recognize what's truly important. Life is about timing. Let this be your time.

Mott-Ohs

If you're standing there waiting for your stars to align, you might want to consider giving them a little nudge.

Life is all about timing. It's all about being in the right place at the right time.

We inherit what we strive and work for in life.

Life's cup of perspective is sure to shock you into a true state of appreciation every time.

CHAPTER 20

TIME TO COOL OFF

The timer is ringing. The cupcakes are done. You can't wait to rip them from the oven. As you rush to remove them, you reach for an oven mitt. It's a subconscious decision, one made without thought. It's a learned behavior that was drilled into your head long ago. "Don't touch that, it's hot!" "Be careful! That will burn you!" "You may want to blow on that before you take a bite." At a very early age, we are taught that *it's best to let things cool down before we touch them*, or especially try to eat them. This may be one of the first lessons that our parents teach us. They teach us this to protect us from harm. Never did I think that I would be drawing a correlation between the simplest of lessons and perhaps one the most complex.

As we grow older, we tend to lose sight of simple lessons. We tend to become cocky and believe that the lessons that we've learned don't apply anymore. Let's face it. In life, things heat up all the time. It could be the pace at work. It could be tensions in relationships. How about dealing with teenagers? Are you kidding me? The first chapter of *How to Deal with Teens* should be "How to Keep the Tea Kettle from Boiling Over." Seriously, teenagers are enough to make your blood boil. These are not the only things that try your patience. I'm sure that you can think of plenty of examples of when the heat has gotten too hot in the kitchen. Have you ever heard that expression "If you can't handle the heat, then get out of the kitchen?" Well, I'd like to modify the old adage slightly to say, *"It's best to get out of the kitchen if the heat is affecting your judgment."*

It makes perfect sense. Have you ever said anything that you wished that you could take back? Maybe you did something in the heat of the moment. When the dust settled, or you had some time to cool down and rationalize things, you really wished you had waited to act or handled it differently. In the game of golf, if you blow your shot, often people use the word "mulligan" instead of the term "do over" to call attention to the fact that someone is going to take a second shot free, without a penalty stroke. Nobody knows for sure where this term came from. However, it's been suggested that it originated in Ireland. "Mulligan" is a very common Irish name, and the common belief is that after hitting a bad shot, a man by the last name of Mulligan decided that he would just shoot again. From that time forward, it has been referred to as a "mully" or a "mulligan"

Unfortunately, life is not always this kind. Life does not always give us multiple opportunities to get things right. Often, there's barely enough time to get it right the first time. Life is not easy. Life is not kind. Life is sometimes just downright hard to deal with in the heat of the moment. It's the heat of the moment that normally trips people up. The heat coerces people into saying and doing things that they wouldn't normally do. Awareness is often half of the battle. If you know that life is going to turn up the heat, why not be prepared to deal with it?

So how do we get prepared? There are really two ways to deal with difficult situations, and they are either "now" or "later." For those situations that are truly emergencies in life, "now" is the only answer. You know these situations. As much as you would like to deal with them later, smoldering issues are sure to grow into fires if left alone. In these cases, the head-on approach is best, but be prepared for the heat. Being prepared is the key to avoiding blunders or saying things that you might regret.

Words are an extremely powerful tool, and they can work for you or against you. Have you ever been surprised by how someone interpreted what you said? Maybe he or she took it out of context. Have you ever been surprised at the impact you have on people through the words that you choose? In my early years of supervising, I had a hot temper. Not as hot as others, but it was hot at times. I often dealt with things head on, and my delivery, although calculated, was probably over the top. Why over the top? Because I failed to calculate the perception of others. We never know what effect our words will have on someone. With those that we supervise, in most cases the impact is huge. If we need to discipline someone or set them straight, any action on a supervisor's part is perceived twice as forcefully on the receiving end. Given that fact, I now ask myself the following: What is my intended message? How is my delivery? I tend to scale back a bit, as I know that my tone will be amplified in the mind of the employee. When the volume is turned down, you are sure to convey your message effectively.

So, how long should we let these cupcakes cool? When is the right time to deal with something? For those of you who are what I like to call "cross it off" people, later is never the time. What is a "cross it off" person? It's the type of person that's all about crossing things off the list. Problem with these folks is that it's often about crossing the item off the list rather than completing the task properly. There's a place and a time to deal with everything. Some things are best left to sit and cool off for a bit.

Over time, I have seen supervisors come and go. On occasion, I have run into supervisors who I thought were slow in dealing with things. They were constantly using inaction when it came to what I thought, at the time, were life-and-death situations. I would be yelling, "Fire! Fire! Rome is burning!" and instead of rushing to the rescue with a bucket or a fire extinguisher, they would be walking in the opposite direction. This inaction used to drive me crazy! Little did I know, these individuals had already played all the scenarios out in their heads. They had arrived at the conclusion that letting time pass might just be the best action. Their perceived inaction was actually a very seasoned and deliberate action.

In the heat of the moment, the best action is sometimes inaction. Think about it. There are those instances that are so intense that if they are dealt with immediately, people are certain to come to blows. Yet if the problem is slept on, the next day, time has diffused the situation. Calmer heads prevail and the problem becomes more manageable. Often I have seen the problem go totally away without any action at all. People often can find perspective after distancing themselves from the intensity of the moment.

I often suggest that clients write down what they would say to a person with whom they are experiencing conflict. Get it all out. Vent your emotions on paper and then fold it up and seal it safely away in an envelope. Go away and sleep on the situation. Read what you wrote in the morning and see if you still feel the same way. Nine times out of ten, you will rip the note up. Can you imagine if all of that had come out of your mouth? Can you imagine what the impact would be? Normally you would have taken a hot situation and turned it into a raging forest fire. With my teenagers I try to stress this the most. Sometimes there's absolutely no filter between what comes into their head and what crosses their lips. The problem with words is that you can never take them back. In life, let things sit. Let them cool down, and then pick your words wisely. Let the cupcakes cool and you're less apt to get burned.

Mott-Ohs

It's really best to let things cool down before we touch them.

It's best to get out of the kitchen if the heat is affecting your judgment.

In the heat of the moment, the best action is sometimes inaction.

CHAPTER 21

ONE CUPCAKE OR TWELVE?

Do you ever catch yourself wishing you just had a bit more than you have right now? Maybe when you were younger, you just wanted to be older. Maybe it was hitting a certain age so you could get a driver's license. Then, it became about getting out of college so you could get a job. At some point, you had wished a good portion of your life away. Then the tide turned and you started wishing that you could go back. Before you know it, you have spent so much time wishing that you were somewhere else that you haven't thoroughly enjoyed where you are.

As Americans, we always want more than we have. Why do you think credit card companies are so wildly successful? Why do you think that there's a financial crisis? Why do you think that our government is in debt? It's all due to society wanting more and finding ways to get it.

Why can't we just be content? I've searched for the answer to this question. I'm as guilty as the next person when it comes to looking ahead, looking back, being envious, and not being content. In the past, I leveraged what I didn't have to obtain what I wanted or thought I needed. Today is a new day. I have changed. I have redesigned my life to cater to the present. I'm content.

We are what we say we are. We become what we think about. Our continuous envy or drive to have more than we currently have can be attributed to confusion.

We are confused when it comes to the definition of need and want. You will often hear people say "I need this" or " I need that" when they really simply just want it. "Need" is defined as something of necessity. It's often something essential to stay alive. Food, shelter, and water are all necessities that one needs. "Want" is something that you desire. It's something that you would like to have but that you can do without. I want two hundred television channels, but I most certainly don't need two hundred channels of infomercials to stay alive. We muddy the waters by confusing the two terms. We confuse ourselves into perceiving that we need things when we really don't. My brother said it best the other day. He was talking about our insatiable appetite for material items. He said, *"We all need to loosen the noose to find our true passion."* This phrase stuck with me as I pondered its true meaning. I came to realize that what my brother was trying to convey is that as we grow older and fall into this never-ending trap of envy, we grow into our lifestyles. As we make more money, we acquire more things in proportion. We really don't ever seem to get ahead, as we just simply have more to deal with.

How many of you have earned that raise and the first thing that you contemplate is how you are going to spend the extra money? In most cases, instead of ridding yourself of financial liabilities and easing the burden, you choose to add more to the mix. This is exactly what my brother was referring to when he mentioned the noose. The noose is the lifestyle that we choose to order up from the universe. Yes, you are in full control of how you live. You are in full control when you decide to spend rather than to save. As you literally buy into the idea that you need something when you really only want it, you only serve to tighten the noose. Why a noose? Because *often people strangle themselves by their own desires.* As we give in to our short-term cravings, we often cut off the path to satiating our long-term desires. After all, life is all about finding our true passion and being able to pursue it. *Our true passion is what ultimately fills our cup of contentment.*

As a result of my most recent attempt to downsize or simplify my life, I am beginning to see that it doesn't take a lot to make me happy. If we silence the noise, it's the smaller things in life that end up speaking to us the loudest. Most of the things that make us happy are not material. When we grasp this, our cup starts to overflow, as the things filling it are available in abundance.

Remember that when it comes to true wealth in the world, it's up to you to define what this means. Only you can set the bar when it comes to reaching your own true happiness in life.

In the last five years, my paradigm has totally shifted. As I have downsized, I have started to loosen the noose. I started to realize that what I was striving for in the first chapter of my life was no longer important to me in what was appearing to be the second. I was always a man that set goals. Sometimes they were financial. Sometimes they were career based. More often than not, they were linked to some material item that would signal to the universe and everyone around me that I was successful. One day, this all shifted. The material things did not matter anymore. What I craved yesterday was not what I was craving today. I was craving more emotionally satisfying things in life. The things that had climbed to the top of my priority list were the love of my family and the healthy relationships with my kids and friends. So rather than pushing to add things into my life, I started to eliminate the things that were not on my priority list. Believe me, this was not at all an easy thing to do. I needed to fight my programmed perceptions of what was right and wrong at every turn. I had to fight the criticism of those around me. Most important, I had to be very focused on what I call the "five-mile view." The five-mile view is something that you have to be able to focus on and identify. It's like having foresight. It's the ability to recognize that there's either a pot of gold or a kettle of coal at the end of the road. It's the ability to see the road ahead and to make course corrections to either head for the prize or avoid the pitfalls.

If only we had binoculars or a crystal ball that would allow us to see five miles down the road. Life would be easier but boring in the same breath. One of life's most attractive qualities is the fact that everything isn't always pre-ordained. Life should be like the night before Christmas, where everyone is eager with anticipation and excited about the possibilities that lie ahead. Are you one of the curious ones? Have you ever stopped to ponder the wonders of the world? Do you always want to discover the "why" in life?

Why is a baseball bat a certain length? Why does beer come in a six-pack? Why does a gross always equal 144? Why do they sell eggs by the dozen?

Or why does the average cupcake pan come equipped to bake twelve cupcakes? Perhaps that question alone should be the eighth wonder of the world. I think not. Perhaps the Ten Commandments had a subsection that read, "Cupcakes are always baked in a pan of twelve." I bet not. However, if there was a subsection of the Ten Commandments devoted just to cupcakes, it would say, *"Cupcakes are made to be shared."* It would also say, *"Too much of anything is a bad thing."*

Allow me to transport you back in time a bit; back to the simple days of elementary school. If there were twenty-four kids in your class, what did that mean? To the average first through fifth grader, it meant that there were twenty-four birthdays to celebrate! Yes, the days when there would be a break from the routine for the sole purpose of celebrating one's birthday and, more importantly, a chance to eat some goodies. More often than not, it was cupcakes. Two batches of twelve made to be shared. "Pass the cupcakes, please." Think back to those days, as your entire face would light up with the thought of "sprinkles on top!" *Everything is better with sprinkles on top!*

We were taught at a very early age that everything is better when shared. Somewhere along the way, this idea seems to diminish. At some point, the tide turns, and instead of a "we" thing, it becomes an "I" thing. "I must have this." "I must have more of this." "I must have it all." When this shift occurs, we start to see the demise of good nature. We see an unhealthy state of scarcity. We start to lose our sprinkles. The world was not meant to have certain people holding a monopoly over the supply of sprinkles. Can you even imagine what the world would be like if we were all just vanilla cupcakes: cupcakes with no icing, no sprinkles, and nothing to set us apart from one another? It's not a world that I would want to live in. In America, our sprinkle supply has diminished, and it's time to crank up the sprinkle production to full speed.

As I mentioned in the introduction, scarcity can be used to create positive momentum in your life. At the same time, it can also create negative momentum. Scarcity created at the expense of others can be detrimental not only to those who lack, but to those who benefit from an unhealthy state of abundance. Take a moment to think about how balanced your life is. If you evaluate the times of trouble in your life, you will find that it's normally caused by a state of unbalance. Somewhere there was an area that had too little or too much. The trouble was caused by focusing on one aspect to the neglect of another.

In life, you are not meant to eat or hoard all twelve cupcakes. Moderation is the key. Sadly, we have lost this idea of moderation. Sadly, we have become one of the most obese and unhealthy nations on the face of the planet. Obesity is rampant in the United States: 3.8 million people are over 300 pounds, over 400,000 people (mostly males) carry over 400 pounds, and the average adult female weighs an unprecedented 163 pounds! Childhood obesity in the United States has more than tripled in the past two decades. If those aren't some staggering, eye-opening statistics that make you stand up and take notice, I don't know what will.

So what's the solution to the problem? The solution is maintaining a balance between mine, yours, and ours. Let's examine them a bit.

Mine: Those that fall into the "mine" trap normally lead very lonely lives as they are always thinking of themselves. When looking back on their lives, most of them would have traded all the money in China to fill the void or eliminate the regret in their lives. It's your choice. You control your own destiny. What do you want your tombstone to read? "He died with everything but he really had nothing!" Or "He lived through moderation, and through moderation he had everything!" How do you want to be remembered? Sir Winston Churchill once said, "We make a living by what we get; we make a life by what we give."

A prime example of greed in America is our favorite diva of the homemaking scene, Martha Stewart. Martha, as you know is a self-made millionaire. No, strike that, she is a billionaire. However, she recently spent five months in prison and to this day passes the blame onto others for her own decision not to be truthful. She fell into the "mine" trap. When is enough really enough? This is a good question, and only you can answer that. I'm here to tell you that enough is enough when you are so focused on yourself that you do unethical things or compromise your basic values. These principles are clearly described in a fantastic book, *All I Really Need to Know I Learned in Kindergarten*, by Robert Fulghum. One of the most important principles outlined in his book is the ability to say "I'm sorry."

What most people don't realize is that Martha Stewart didn't go to jail for insider trading. She went to jail for lying to officials. Had she admitted that she was aware insider trading had occurred, she could have avoided jail time. She was convicted for conspiracy, obstruction of an agency proceeding, and making false statements to federal investigators. Her behavior, which defied simple principles of what is right and wrong, was bad but was not illegal. Her decision to lie to officials was stupidity at its best! It was her lack of honesty that landed her in prison. She had everything and compromised her own integrity for the sake of "mine." She was so in the "mine" phase that it cost her five months out of her life.

We must learn from our mistakes. I recently watched Martha Stewart in an interview, and even though she's had much time to analyze the events, she still believes that she is blameless. Let's not be like Martha Stewart. Much like the obesity problem striking America, we must take accountability. We could blame it on all the fast-food restaurants, but who chooses to drive through them? We do! We could blame it on the food companies, but who chooses to buy that bag of chips or box of cookies? We do! We are to blame. It's too bad that Martha Stewart isn't standing up and taking accountability for her poor decision. This is where I'm suggesting that when we burn the cupcakes, we truly learn the real lessons and take accountability for our actions. Being the queen of the kitchen, Martha, of all people, should have learned something from her mistake.

Dale E. Turner, a famous author, once said, "It is the highest form of self-respect to admit our errors and mistakes and make amends for them. To make a mistake is only an error in judgment, but to adhere to it when it is discovered shows infirmity of character."

Yours: When I talk about "yours," I refer to those things that are possessed by others. We are so often consumed with the idea of how much others have in life. Why does it matter? Is there really a shortage of anything that's truly important? When you waste time thinking of what others have, you only take away from the time you have to enjoy. Time is truly important. Envy is not. Time may be the one thing that there's a shortage of, depending on when your time is up.

A wealthy world is one in which there is true abundance for all. Unfortunately, we are far from that world. When I can travel to any city in the United States and find people sleeping on the streets no matter what the temperature, we are far from abundance. *The definition of abundance should be: I have mine, you have yours, and together we can come together to pledge ours to others.* Together we can make the world one of abundance.

Ours: Can you imagine if some of the most amazing things in life were owned or were exclusively used by just a few? Imagine that one man owned Yosemite National Park. Imagine if he placed a fence around the entire park so nobody could see the magnificent treasures that it holds, such as Half Dome and Yosemite Falls. Imagine if Niagara Falls was owned by one person who decided to ban any visitors to save all the rainbows for himself. How wasteful would this be? Some things in life are surely meant to be shared.

When we are young, being selfish is almost a given. As we mature, our selfish feelings shift from excitement on our own behalf to excitement for others. The gift of receiving turns into the gift of giving. What was once mine became ours and, even more, yours. For me it shifted early on when I started to make things for my parents in school. Maybe it was that glitter-covered pinecone or that ceramic bowl. Maybe it was that clothes pin reindeer or the plaster hand print. It wasn't really the material item at all, but rather the time that was vested in thinking of others. *Time spent thinking of the well-being of others is time never wasted.* It was time spent thinking of another person that turned the tide. Once you start to invest your time in others, their happiness rather than your own becomes the new priority. The "ours" idea is the polar opposite of the "mine" idea. Mark Twain once said, "Kindness is the language which the deaf can hear and the blind can see." Giving and sharing with one another is a universal language. I have always said that *charity with the expectation of nothing in return is sure to warm your heart and feed the soul.*

"Thousands of candles can be lit from a single candle, and the life of the candle will not be shortened. Happiness never decreases by being shared."—Buddha

Mott-Ohs

We are what we say we are. We become what we think about.

We all need to loosen the noose to find our true passion.

Often people strangle themselves by their own desires.

Our true passion is what ultimately fills our cup of contentment.

Cupcakes are made to be shared.

Too much of anything is a bad thing.

Everything is better with sprinkles on top!

The definition of abundance should mean that I have mine, you have yours, and together we can come together to pledge ours to others.

Time spent thinking of the well-being of others is time never wasted.

Charity with the expectation of nothing in return is sure to warm your heart and feed the soul.

CHAPTER 22

FROST YOURSELF

What did you want to be growing up? Was it a firefighter, a doctor, or maybe a police officer? Was it possibly something different? No matter what it was, there really was no question whether you would achieve it or not. You simply made it so in your head and "poof," all your dreams came true. There was never anyone standing in your way, nobody suggesting that you couldn't be who you wanted to be. Dreaming big was encouraged. *In our youth, no courage was needed, for there was never any doubt.*

How do your aspirations from childhood compare to your reality today? If you were asked the same question today, would you answer the same way as you did then? Individuals rarely know early in life what they want to be when they grow up. Most of us are a work in progress and find our true calling later on in life. Regardless of the timing, individuals are like flowers. Whether you bloom early in the season or late, all are destined to bloom. Everyone is beautiful in his or her own and very distinct way.

Deciding who you want to be and truly blooming into the real you is the very least that you deserve in life. There is no shame in grabbing the brass ring. There is no shame in living happily ever after. *The only shame in life is failing to realize your true potential.* I have given the flavor vanilla a ton of flack throughout the book. Vanilla has simply been sacrificed in my analogies to stress the importance of straying from the norm. "Who would ever want to be vanilla?" To be honest, I am a big fan of vanilla. After all, what would apple pie be without vanilla ice cream? What would the wafer be without the vanilla? What would the hot fudge sundae be without the base of vanilla ice cream? Vanilla has a very subtle but distinct taste to it and often makes everything taste just a bit better.

No matter what flavor you choose to be, you must frost yourself. I'm sure that you have all heard the expression "Everything else is icing on top of the cake!" It's so true when applied to life. After you achieve your goal, everything past that is a bonus. It's a treat. The treats are the fruits of your labor. You have committed to the plan. You have stuck to your conviction. You have loved, laughed, cried, and learned along the way.

We have spent this entire book thinking and contemplating. What's the right mixture to find your true destiny in life? By now, you should have all the ingredients necessary. Your kitchen should be equipped with all the tools and the support system necessary to assist you in baking the perfect batch of cupcakes. Now it's time to celebrate your success. It's time to frost yourself! It's time to return to those years where you dreamed the dream and your dreams were reality.

We have worked so hard in the kitchen to ensure that you have the foundation to bake up something great. It's now your time to treat yourself in the way that you did when you were young. You are unstoppable. There is no tree that you cannot climb. No creek that you can't cross. You're not fearful of failure, as failure does not exist. There's nothing that you can't accomplish. Your mind is all powerful, and if you dream it, it will be so. Now is the time to treat yourself with a renewed level of respect. There is no person or thing that you put higher on the pedestal than yourself. Yes, people may be at the same level, but you only look up to one person, yourself, or to a higher power. Gone are the days that someone or something can bring you down a notch. Gone are the days that we listen to the Wah Wah Bes. Gone are the days that we listen to that voice of doubt on our shoulder. Our head is clear and our life is filled with positive vibrations that overpower anything that interferes with our tune.

You are you. You are unique. You are special. You are one of a kind. You are the icing on the cake. You are the king or queen of your kitchen. You just whipped up a new batch of self-respect. Go frost yourself!

Confucius once said, "Respect yourself and others will respect you."

Mott-Ohs

In our youth, no courage was needed, for there was never any doubt.

The only shame in life is failing to realize your true potential.

CHAPTER 23

SAVOR EVERY BITE!

As I write this, I'm sitting at a bar in the midafternoon. The hustle and bustle of the world is spinning by me. The bartender is shaking some kind of mixed drink as the waitress waits patiently. The fine gentlemen to my left is attempting to make idle conversation. Over the past few years, I have really mastered the art of slowing things down and observing the smaller things around me. By doing so, I have come to savor every bite that life has to offer. However, at this moment, all I can think of is the day's events, which were truly just an exclamation point on an amazing week. I'm writing with a flurry. *When your idea cup overflows, it's best to pour as fast as you possibly can.*

My morning started by dropping my youngest son at school after spending seven intense days with my soon-to-be-eighty–year-old father. I spent the week with him as a pet project. This pet project deserves some backstory. As I mentioned in the introduction, my father is a very dynamic fellow. He was my hero early on in life. He was definitely a man to admire. He was funny, charismatic, and could instantly take command of any room without the use of firearms. He had a zest for life that was unsurpassed. However, at some point in life, I realized that he was just a man. He was just a mere mortal like the rest of us. He was capable of making the same mistakes and had his own set of issues. Putting all this aside, he was still my mortal hero.

At some point, my blind admiration changed. I guess it was shortly after my mom passed. Dad made either the conscious or unconscious decision to check out. On one hand, who could blame him? His soul mate of almost fifty years had just passed away at the hands of cancer. I can only imagine how that would have rocked my foundation. I can remember the pain I experienced from losing my mom. For my dad, he had lost his best friend. However, how could he choose something other than to push on in life? How could my hero of the past make the decision of a coward? Why would he choose not to make the most of life and savor every bite that his family had to offer? After all, his wife's life was cut short. He of all people should realize how precious every minute is and was. This is the point when I realized what real courage was in life. *It takes real courage to live when life feels like it's not worth living.*

Believe it or not, this went on for almost ten years. There were attempts to rescue him, but they were weak at best. We were all dealing with our own personal grief. He eventually moved in with me after a prize fight between his Jeep Wrangler and a gigantic pine tree. He still, to this day, has a quarter-size indentation in his head from that unconscious attempt at offing himself. Eventually, I had had enough. I couldn't keep driving three hours to the foothills of California to rescue him. The obvious thing to do was to have him move in with me. Now that I look back, it was as much for me as it was for him. He and I were both swirling at the same time—he, from the loss of his soul mate, and I, from the loss of what I thought was mine, and my mom's death all at the same time. I was both the best and the worst person to move in with, as I could barely take care of my own kitchen. Needless to say, the doors to our pantries were facades at best. Our pantries were a mess and we were adding all the wrong ingredients into our lives to mask the pain associated with our loss.

Fast-forward ten years and we're looking at a very old eighty-year-old. Isn't that redundant, "very old" and "eighty years old"? Nope, not really. Anyone, no matter the age, has a true effective age. In real estate, the term is used to refer to the wear and tear that a piece of property has endured. In the case of my father, his effective age was much older than his actual age. He had made some poor choices that added to his personal wear and tear. He was an on again, off again smoker, and he struggled with his weight from time to time. When things started to get rough, when his foundation crumbled, he retreated to his poor habits and adopted even more. Smoking, overeating, and a sedentary lifestyle, all combined with depression, eventually led to a state of atrophy. Atrophy is a term used to describe the partial or complete wasting away of a part of the body. In the case of my father, he had been shutting down for years. He had given up. It wasn't just a single part of his body but rather his entire being that was wasting away. His life was sliding into a complete state of atrophy.

It's a waste that at the point of his life when his radius of opportunity was infinitely endless, he decided to live in a cocoon. He literally lived in a radius that consisted of a square mile. All of his activity at home consisted of walking either to the bathroom or the kitchen. Everywhere else he achieved by car. Most of his time was spent lying in bed. Can you even imagine what that would do to your body? For most of us, if we come down with an illness and lie in bed for more than a day, our bodies ache from the sedentary state. Can you imagine ten years of that? People would ask me how my father was, and I would tell them, "He's waiting to die." It may sound harsh, but there was resentment there. How could he make the decision of a coward, which was to stop living? How could he choose not to savor every bite? He of all people should have realized through loss that life is so precious. *Every minute is a gift.* At some point, I woke up and realized that my judgment of him was highly hypocritical. After all, I had checked out in the same way after I lost Mom and my wife. I was just fortunate to pull myself out of the hole.

After I had healed, I hit a point where I couldn't stand by and watch my father decompose in front of me. There had been attempts to jump-start his batteries before, but this time was going to be different. I called him on the phone and said simply this: "I want my Dad back." I then paused and there was dead silence on the other end of the phone. I then said, "I'll give you seven days of my time if you give me seven of yours." I then encouraged him to think it over for a bit and get back to me. His response was, "I don't need time to think about it, I'm in!" So my pet project was born. Game on! I had crossed one critical hurdle, which was to gain his acceptance, but now on to the logistics of getting him down the rest of the track. I choose the track analogy because, in his high school days, my father was one fast runner. He held the state record in the low hurdles until they changed the format of the race. How do you bring a person back from a state of atrophy? How do I find that championship athlete in him at age eighty? That was the mission, but the true goal was to help him find his sprinkles again. The true goal was to get my dad back!

It was an amazing week, filled with its high points and its fair share of challenges. After all, it really was an intervention. Not the norm, but an intervention with an eighty-year-old that was very set in his ways. I literally had to grab my father's hand and lead him out of the land of darkness that he had created for himself. I showed him the way, but he had to both initiate and take the journey step by step. It had to be his choice. I won't go into all the details of how we did it, other than to say we restructured his life from top to bottom. We examined routines that had become ruts. We redesigned them to promote a healthy and positive direction. We focused on eliminating all the negative ingredients and the triggers in his life. For clarification, triggers are stimuli that flip an unconscious switch in your head to promote your bad habits. For instance, I asked my dad what specific things caused him to smoke. He responded with the following: stress, boredom, coffee, food, alcohol, and sex, of all things. Okay, the last one was enough to make me walk out on day one! Sex and your parents don't ever mix, I don't care how old you are!

Back on track and onto the triggers...

Stress: How possibly could an eighty-year-old be stressed? Believe it or not, this age demographic worries about everything. It's proven that they worry more than any other age bracket. He would lie in his room watching the news all day. I would return from work and the first words out of his mouth were, "Did you hear about this tragedy?" "Did you hear this person shot this person?" I finally got to the point where I told him not to talk to me unless he had some good news to talk about. I don't know about you, but I personally need to search for good news during each broadcast to find something positive. It was a recipe for disaster. News plus worry equals stress. So the first thing we did was to design a day that didn't revolve around the news. His morning normally started by reading the paper. We enabled him by placing it at his door. When he woke up it would be right there. No more. I relocated the paper to the kitchen upstairs and threw everything away but the sports section. I can still hear him: "Where the hell is my paper!" "Come and get it, Big Boy! It's right up here." He wasn't happy, to say the least, and when he received just the sporting news, he was even more upset. I explained to him that there was some method to my madness. Why read something that's normally depressing and that's one of the causes of his worries? Why would you purposely insert a smoking trigger into your routine? I replaced it with a positive talk show on morning television. It just happened to be *Live with Regis and Kelly*. This was not just by chance. Regis is almost the identical age to my father. Yet he has a positive command on his life. He has made the choice to make the most of things. This was a living, breathing example of what I was searching to find in my father.

Boredom: This was easy. He led a sedentary life. Instead of taking from the universe, we decided to give back and structured his lifestyle around the nearby senior center. It was five minutes down the street. However, due to his shrinking radius and outlook on life, he had never been there in ten years. For those of you with aging parents, senior centers are normally fantastic places. They have caring volunteers, wonderful activities, and what I consider as one our nation's most wasted and underappreciated resources—senior citizens. *Spend an hour really listening to a senior and you will have walked miles through a fascinating life.* After all, they have been there and done that. They have made their mistakes and learned from them. They really get what life is all about and truly savor every bite. *Getting involved and having a purpose to your day is essential at any age.* This was a critical ingredient when it came to completing the formula for Dad's recovery. It was essential that he be around people his age who truly had their sprinkles. He needed to feed off theirs to find his again.

Coffee: No, we didn't take away his coffee, but we did move it back in the morning routine. Move it back? Most of you are getting the shakes just thinking about it. My girlfriend is one of those people. Once she breaches the morning, she makes a beeline for the coffee pot. For those who would make the mistake of crossing her path, it might just be the last mistake that you make. Get in her way and it's "Murder, death, kill! Murder, death, kill!" It would be like stepping between a momma bear and her cub. The carnage wouldn't be pretty. Her routine was much like my dad's. Despite how strange of an idea that it may seem, this was a critical step in starting the day off on the right foot. Everyone should be consuming the proper amount of water per day. For most of us this is a challenge. It's a challenge because we mostly drink after feeling dehydrated. The morning is a prime example of this. We awaken in a state of dehydration. The problem is that most of us make a poor decision when it comes to quenching our thirst. We reach for a cup of coffee for the associated pick-me-up, satisfy the urge, and continue to navigate through the day without any water consumption. Again, I'm not saying that you should not have coffee. Most things, if they are taken in moderation, are okay. All I'm saying is that you might consider doing what we did for Dad. Instead of going right to the coffee machine, I sent him in pursuit of one glass of water and a half glass of orange juice. In order for him to have his first cup of the day, he had to consume both. This was interesting in many ways. Not only was I inserting healthier ingredients into the beginning of his day, but at the same time, I was teaching him the difference between "want" and "need." He had made his body believe that he needed coffee, filled with artificial sweetener and a bunch of other junk, while the only thing he needed was water. He wanted coffee due to some unsophisticated urges brought to him by the bad little man sitting on his shoulder. He convinced himself, and eventually his brain, that it was a necessity. Just as the need was fabricated, it could be deconstructed. After he had the initial cup of water and orange juice, the feeling of dehydration subsided and the need diminished. The need for coffee was reduced simply to a minor want.

Alcohol: This was easy, too. We determined that the time Dad was most likely to drink was late at night. It was normally when everyone else was drinking as a way to fit into the group. The solution was to keep him busy and tire him out. I kept him moving all the time so he couldn't stay up late enough to join in any of the drinking activities.

Food: When it came to food, this was a bigger deal. We had to transform a diet that consisted of danishes, doughnuts, and fast food into a healthy routine. It had to be nutritious, satisfying, and feasible. When tailoring an eating plan for an individual, you must know your audience. In this case, Dad is a senior. Risking generalizations, I'd estimate that most seniors are path-of-least-resistance people. They very rarely will spend the time to prepare a complex meal. I solicited help from my sister, an international nutrition and fitness expert, and away we went. She designed a meal plan and then took us to the store to teach us about the dos and don'ts of shopping. We got him on track with food choices. To curb cravings for a cigarette, we set up a walking routine after each meal. It took his mind totally off that after-meal fixation, and he quit with ease.

I believe the primary reason people have such a hard time breaking bad habits is that they just try to quit cold turkey. They fail to identify the triggers that foster the habit. It's so critical to identify the triggers. You may have the will and commitment, but without looking at the root cause of the addiction and the triggers, you are stacking the cards against yourself. You need to remove yourself from the negative routine or rut that led you there. You need to surround yourself with positive ingredients to foster your success and the ultimate change.

As I said, the week was amazing. We made so much progress. I set my bar for the week and Dad jumped over it with ease. He exceeded my expectations in every category. In one power-packed week, Dad lost seven pounds, stopped smoking, improved his vision due to not being dehydrated, got involved at the senior center, improved his sleeping habits, and is now walking a mile a day rather than grabbing for a cigarette or a doughnut. He's on track! What's more important, he's savoring every healthy bite of life and we found his sprinkles again. Check out the difference from day one to day seven.

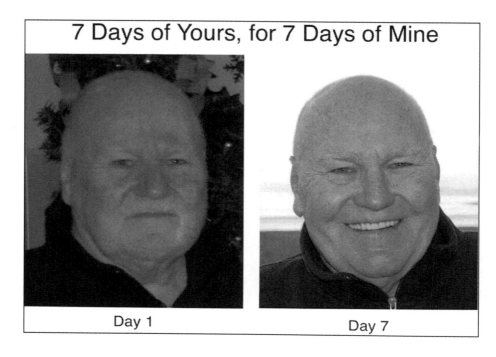

7 Days of Yours, for 7 Days of Mine

Day 1   Day 7

Can you see what I am talking about? Do you see how in the day one picture to the left that it's almost as if he is crying from the inside. With not even saying a word, he is yelling for someone to come to his rescue. His entire face and being is saying that he doesn't want to be in the space that he has created for himself. He had lost his sprinkles! The day seven photo, on the other hand, is a complete transformation. His eyes are clear, complexion is better, and he looks like he has it again. That's my dad! He has his sprinkles again! It takes six weeks to form the habits that we introduced in our first seven days together. There may be setbacks, but we're prepared for that and motivated to accomplish what we set out to do. *We have renewed purpose, backed by commitment, and we are on a mission!*

The week was a success, to say the least. However, it didn't end there. Life just has a way of throwing the unexpected at you. I returned from my dad crusade and landed at my girlfriend, Andrea's, house. More backstory is needed at this moment. Andrea, my girlfriend, recently moved her mother in with her, as she is suffering from cancer. She has struggled with cancer on and off for almost two decades. Most recently, the disease has decided to raise the stakes. It's been taking a toll on her strength, but cannot and will not dampen her spirit. I admire her attitude and fortitude daily. She truly gets the concept of savoring every bite.

She has reached the point where it's necessary to be in an environment where there are caring, watchful eyes. The right solution was to have her move in with Andrea to ensure that she receives the proper care. She has been taking some aggressive amounts of chemotherapy and, as a result, her hair has started to fall out. As you can imagine, it had reached a point at which her appearance was suffering. The afternoon that I returned, Andrea was taking her to buy a wig. Again, another right decision, as your appearance when you are battling a major illness can either work for you or against you. Currently it was working totally against her. She did not look well, and many of us can only imagine the emotional experience for a woman to pull a handful of hair from her head. For men, we can easily shave our heads and blend in with the general population, but for woman, hair is an integral part of their identity. It is intertwined with how feminine they feel. To have it go away can severely dampen one's resolve.

Sandy, Andrea's mom, came into the room where I was working and she asked me, "Chris, would you mind shaving off the rest of my hair?" I was shocked that she asked me the question. I responded quickly and said, "Absolutely, let's do it!" Allow me to clarify. I don't cut hair. The last time I cut someone's hair, my boys were so young that they didn't know any better. I gave them buzz cuts in the garage. I just figured, how could you go wrong shaving it down to almost nothing? However, when I grabbed the shears, it hit me as to what I was about to do. It was almost as if my late mother, who had passed at the hands of cancer herself, placed her hand on my shoulder. She made me pause and ponder the gravity of what I was about to do for Sandy. She wanted to ensure that I would handle the situation with the utmost care and responsibility. There are times that present you with the opportunity to have an impact on the lives of others. This was one of those situations. As Helen Keller once said, "I long to accomplish a great and noble task, but it is my chief duty to accomplish small tasks as if they were great and noble."

As I rounded the corner to the kitchen, Sandy was sitting there with a pair of scissors in hand attempting to cut the hair off herself. She was visibly frustrated and worried about making a mess on the kitchen floor. I gently removed the scissors from her hand and said, "Don't you worry about a thing. Are you ready for your new image? After all, this is the first day of your new life." This was about to be a game changer when it came to how she was feeling about things.

As I was carefully shaving her head, I couldn't stop thinking how significant this event was for Sandy. What a privilege it was. She felt comfortable enough with me to ask me to cut her hair. She was concerned with the new look, as she had lost her hair while fighting a previous bout with breast cancer. She believed that she didn't have a nicely shaped head. To the contrary, she had a great-shaped head, and I let her know it! Compared to what she looked like when I came into the house, she looked absolutely fantastic sporting her newly shaved style. As I put the final touches on what she was calling a masterpiece, I gave her head a bit of a rubdown. *Often in life, it's not about what we say, but rather what we do.* Physical contact often speaks volumes, and the power of touch has been proven to help those struggling with major illness. This was my way of saying to Sandy that she was beautiful in so many ways.

After we were done, Sandy retreated to her own space, and I went back to my neutral corner to absorb what had just happened. As I sat there quietly, my emotions started to take hold. Memories of my mom in the final moments of her life came flooding back. I was so touched that I could share that moment with Sandy that tears started to come to my eyes. Before I broke into a full-on crying session, Sandy broke the silence and thanked me again. I returned that thank you and conveyed what a privilege it was to be of assistance. I am a firm believer that we are a walking reflection of those that we have loved in life and that are no longer with us. The love that I felt that day was the love for both my mother and for Sandy. It was a very special experience, to say the least.

Life seems to speed on by, and before you know it days, weeks, and months have passed in the blink of an eye. We often take life and all its greatness for granted. This is not often intentional. We seem to get caught up in the process. Unlike baking, which is defined in its steps, process, and duration, life isn't the same. Yes, there's an average lifespan, just as there's a suggested baking period. However, life can be cut short at anytime. I ask you this: if you knew that you only had seven days to live, seven bites left, would you treat the days or bites differently? The answer to the question is most assuredly yes. So the true question is, why are you wasting bites of the cupcake? Why are you not savoring every step in the process? Every moment, step, or bite in life is meant to be savored. *After the oven shuts down, it's always easier to remember the bites savored than those squandered. Savor every bite!*

Mott-Ohs

When your idea cup overflows, it's best to pour as fast as you possibly can.

It takes real courage to live when life feels like it's not worth living.

Spend an hour really listening to a senior and you will have walked miles through a fascinating life.

Getting involved and having purpose to your day is essential at any age.

Every minute is a gift.

We have renewed purpose, backed by commitment, and we are on a mission!

Often in life, it's not about what we say, but rather what we do.

After the oven shuts down, it's always easier to remember the bites savored than those squandered. Savor every bite!

CHAPTER 24

BRING ON THE SPRINKLES

I find it fitting that for the last chapter of this book, I have returned to the very place that life really started for me. I was born in Long Branch, New Jersey, and moved to California when I was two years old, spending many of my younger years there. As I mentioned, when I was most impressionable, my mom and dad moved me into the backwoods of Pennsylvania. I have returned to the very place that my parents had taken me when I was thirteen. Time has passed. This just happens to be the thirtieth anniversary of my arrival. Just as a batch is placed in the oven, I too needed to bake for a time. Wow, where did the time go? I came to this magical place as a student. I left as a young man, and now I return as a student again. I have changed, and changed again, but it hasn't. It's still as calm and pristine as ever. We all must find these places in life. These are the places that turn boys into men and then from men to boys again. Whether they are formed in our head or they actually exist, these are our happy places. They are the places where our happiest thoughts and memories lie. These are the quiet places where our spirit is truly born. These are the serene places where we find our true selves. These are the magical and sometimes mystical places from which our sprinkles emerge.

These are the places where we learn to navigate and drive our way through life. In fact, I learned to drive my first automobile, a CJ 7 Jeep Laredo, out on a frozen lake in the dead of winter. Most people find an open parking lot. My parking lot just happened to be a lake with two feet of ice on it. You would imagine, having learned to drive on such a slippery surface, that I would have done better in life when I lost traction. The fact is, I made just as many mistakes as the next person.

I return to this special place that I call PennCrest yearly. I go to walk the woods and to listen to the magic of silence. As I mentioned earlier, great clarity is found in the midst of silence. I go to collect my thoughts and find my center again. *Everything in life emanates from center; it's best to take care of yours.* I return to visit one of the best bakers on the planet. Her name is Lois Hinkley. She is creeping up on the age of eighty-three, yet she's younger than any of us in spirit. She is less than five feet tall and shrinking by the day. What she lacks in height, she makes up for in stature. I often tease Lois that when she leaves the planet, I truly believe that she won't pass away, rather, she will just disappear in a cloud of glory. After all, isn't that how angels depart? She is, without a doubt, one of life's living angels. I am fortunate enough to call her "my second mom."

Lois lives on approximately 150 acres of the most majestic Pennsylvania woodlands. She lives in a meticulously maintained farmhouse that's 176 years old. The furniture is, for the most part, the same as when I arrived thirty years ago. The walls are bare and there's not a picture to be found except for those sitting on a desk. The entire house screams of simplicity and a recipe born out of positive routines. These are the routines built on the premise of "do now" versus "do later." She lives by the philosophy that we only need what we need and all the rest is frivolous. She is perfectly fine to exist on five channels of television, and if a passing storm were to knock out reception, she would simply find something else to occupy her time. All of her set routines promote compound positive ascents in life. There is not a rut to be found unless it exists out on the muddy road leading into the property. Even then, Lois will complain about its mere existence. She knows that *there is no room for ruts in life.* She has little time for those things or people who slow her down. Everything and everyone is always in its place. Her kitchen is always in order and always equipped with the ingredients to bake the perfect batch of cupcakes. She said to me the other day, "I absolutely hate it when I need something and I don't have it." She is a firm believer in being well prepared for whatever life throws at her.

Without fail, Lois wakes up every morning at 4 a.m. At this point, she has what she refers to as her "first breakfast." Then rain, snow, or shine, she enters the dark of the morning to feed a group of fifteen or twenty deer. Her faithful following of woodland creatures are always on time, waiting eagerly in anticipation for their morning portion of corn. If the deer could knock on the door, they probably would. They literally wait right outside her door for her arrival. They would eat from the palm of her hand if allowed. However, that privilege is reserved for one specific deer. This deer is nicknamed "Moocher." Moocher is a survivor. This very recognizable doe has been visiting Lois every morning for approximately fifteen years. Moocher has survived many a hunting season, so she deserves an extra piece of hot dog bun served from the palm of an angel. Being placed on Lois's "A-list" is not an easy thing to achieve. Survivor or not, deer or human, you need to be made of good ingredients and most of all, you need to have something special. You must have your sprinkles.

After starting her day on a good karma footing, Lois goes hard to work on a self-imposed list of duties, only to stop frequently along the way to refuel her tank. She will eat more snacks and or meals in the morning hours than most of us will during a day. This just goes to prove that if you stay active in life, you can eat whatever you want within reason. I truly believe that Mother Nature throws a bit of inclement weather into Lois's mix just to slow her down a bit. She will not rest until the list in her head is complete.

Until ten years ago, Lois was married to her soul mate, Gordon. Gordon and Lois met in their teens. They were hired as caretakers to run an overall estate of three hundred acres, which included a working Christmas tree farm. They were originally hired at a rate of ten cents per hour, just to add a bit of perspective. Lois and Gordon never attended college. Gordon dropped out of school before completing high school. The more amazing statistic was that he was kicked out of the house at age ten and told to go make a living. Can you imagine kicking your ten-year-old out the door? Maybe you can. Maybe you have wanted to, perhaps dreamed about it, but most people would never really do it. Without a doubt, that was a different era. It was shortly after the Great Depression and people were very aware of the difference between need and want. People rarely focused on thoughts of want, as the reality of need consumed their days to survive. Gordon and Lois were individuals that had taken the hard road, and it wasn't necessarily by choice. They were not school smart. They were life smart beyond imagination. Mom and Dad, whether they knew it or not at the time, had just added two master bakers to my kitchen.

Instead of just Dad and Mom, I now had Gordon and Lois Hinkley. *I truly believe that behind every shining star in life, there is a great coach.* In my case, I had a stellar coaching staff: my mom to teach me the true art of life's philanthropy, my father to teach me a sense of humor and the art of selling, and then there were Gordon and Lois. They bestowed a work ethic that was unparalleled. They showed me that a man could find solace in a joyful and honest day's work. My first job, at age thirteen, was to assist Gordon and Lois on the Christmas tree farm. "An honest day's work" was an understatement. I still have the scars to prove it. In the summer, we would sheer trees in very hot and humid weather. In the winter, we would cut trees in some bone-chilling temperatures. Regardless of the weather, regardless of the task, it was sincerely a pleasure to work alongside Gordon and Lois. They approached each day and each job with such passion. They truly loved each other and loved the life that they were living. They treated work as something they wanted to do rather than something that they had to do. They were slaves to no man and were there for their own reasons and no others.

Study those that are truly successful. Ask them how they arrived and they will tell you it's because they truly love what they do in life. More important, they truly love themselves. In order for the world to appreciate your true sprinkles, you must find them first. In order for you to find them, you need to find a life where you are truly content. You must find your purpose. Your purpose is your true passion in life. Pure passion fuels the sprinkle tank. You need to love who you are and what you do. The definition of how you achieve that goal is entirely in the palm of your hand. When I asked Lois just the other day what the secret to a happy life was, without hesitation, she used one word, "variety." Just as we discussed in the "Mix It Up" chapter, there has to be the right mixture in life. You must mix things up.

Life can't be about just one single thing. It's amazing to me that in our younger years, we're constantly surrounded by coaches. Then, later in life, we tend to rely less on coaches. It may just be that the time that we choose to cast away our coaches is actually the time when we need them the most. As our lives tend to pull us in multiple directions, we lose sight of variety in life. Coaches help us maintain that balance and variety to which Lois was referring. Every star player, despite his or her age, should have the strongest life coach.

Have you ever noticed that some people just have that sparkle in their eye, maybe that spring in their step, or that never-ending smile? They seem to be the epitome of the Energizer Bunny. Gordon and Lois were and still are these people. I mention present and past tenses, as Lois is still going strong. Gordon, on the other hand, passed away just before my mom. In fact, I didn't find out about Gordon's passing until I had called to inform them of mother's illness. To this day, I sincerely regret not knowing of one of my life coaches' passing. *It's ever so important to pay attention in life.* It's even more important to stay in touch constantly with those that we love and cherish. Life sometimes takes hold of us, and if we're not strong enough, we can easily be swept away. This was one of these instances in my life. I was not paying attention, and as a result I will forever live with this regret. I have forgiven myself for my ignorance. But it will forever serve as a wake-up call as to the importance of life's vigilance.

When it came to Gordon and Lois, there was never a day that grass grew beneath their feet. I suppose that's why I return on an annual basis. It's truly inspiring to watch. Those artificial injections of energy that people have grown accustomed to are nowhere to be found. Lois keeps going, going, and going. She has never-ending energy and enthusiasm. Her zest for life and outlook are contagious. Yup, this is it. This is the state that we have been talking about. This is what you want and need in life. These are the sprinkles. Often we look at these individuals in amazement and awe. It's not a momentary thing. It's not a passing thought. It's a constant state of being. You can almost feed off the energy that these folks send out to the universe.

It's not coincidence that everyone wants to be around these people. These people are the true power brokers in life. I'm not talking about assets or money. Instead of having it all, they have just what they need in all the right areas. They have that killer hand that is sure to win any poker game: the royal flush. They have the connections that allow them to skip to the front of the line. They have found the golden ticket. They are sprinkle brokers. Why? It's not because they have superior intelligence. It's not because they were born with the silver spoon in their mouth, and it's surely not by luck. It's due to one reason and one only: their kitchen is in order. They have all the right ingredients. They have powerful bakers surrounding them, and their kitchen is baking the perfect mixture that translates into the best batch in life. They have their sprinkles. Each and every one of them has it in his or her own way. It's unique and tailored to fit. It emanates from his or her center.

This type of energy, this zest for living, can't be bought. It can't be bottled. It can't be found in some store or on some shelf. Sprinkles don't come off the assembly line. They are not cheap and shortcuts can't be taken to obtain them. If you have ever bought a book claiming to make you an instant millionaire, take it back and ask for a refund. If you have ever bought a product promising you the instant cureall, throw it away. There's no miracle cure for whatever ails you in life. You must apply the pothole test to whatever is not working. You must find the cracks and dig deep to where your foundation has been compromised. You have to apply the recipe that we have been discussing to whatever you're looking to fix. It may be wealth, health, happiness, and the list goes on. Whatever it is that you seek, if you simply follow life's baking instructions, you are sure to find what you are looking for in life. If you then add a pinch of enthusiasm, your own contribution of sprinkles, you will, without a doubt, realize true success.

You may be able to buy the spark, but you will never be able to buy the fire. Just as you would buy spark plugs to get a machine to start, you then need the gas to keep the engine running. Life's gas is home grown, plain and simple. Life's machine is fueled by sprinkles. Sprinkles are obtained by following life's instructions. You must pay attention. You must use your senses to discover life's directionals. You must stay vigilant. Obtaining sprinkles is not reserved for the rich. Nor is it simply for the poor. There's an infinite supply, and if you follow your moral compass, there will never be a shortage. Sprinkles are truly the largest untapped natural resource in the universe. It's up to you to go out and get them. *Sprinkles are always within your reach.*

So what exactly are sprinkles? Do they fall from the sky in stormy weather? Possibly. Are they something that you add to food to spice things up a bit? Possibly. Are they the traditional topping on a cupcake? Possibly. However, as we close down the final chapter of the book, they should represent a whole lot more. Sprinkles are not tangible. You can't touch them; rather, they touch you in a profound way. In fact, the center for infectious substances has proclaimed sprinkles to be the most infectious substance on the planet. They are highly contagious! Yes, that's right. Much like the smile that spurs a positive biochemical reaction within the body, sprinkles do the same. Sprinkles send a message to the universe that you have arrived. You get it. Once the universe knows you're ready, it responds by opening up numerous doors in front of you. You may have wondered in the past why good fortune happens to so many "on track" people. This is no coincidence. Good fortune doesn't find them; rather, they find true fortune. They find true fortune by finding their sprinkles in life.

Sprinkles, you can catch just about anywhere or anytime in your lifetime. The downside: there is no cure! Life can attempt to blow out your flame, it can throw potholes in your path, it can try to derail your train, but it can never take away your sprinkles once you've discovered them. It's simply your choice.

One of my favorite scenes of all time was in the movie *A Christmas Carol*. In the movie, Ebenezer Scrooge is visited by three ghosts on Christmas Eve. These ghosts that represent his past, present, and future take Ebenezer on a journey to show him the error of his ways. He had become hardened by life. Through a series of events, he had departed from some of his core beliefs. He allowed cracks in his road to eat away at his moral foundation. He had strayed from his center. He had lost his sprinkles and had grown old and weary. Just as life does, it brought Ebenezer full circle. Life gave him the opportunity to reboot. Reboot he did! As Ebenezer woke on Christmas morning, he realized that the ghosts had spared him. They had given him a second chance. In a scene in cinematic history that I personally will never forget, Ebenezer found his sprinkles again. Giggling without control, Ebenezer realized the error in his ways and wasn't about to waste the opportunity. He sprung out of bed with a spring in his step and a smile on his face. He was determined to rewrite his story and leave a positive footprint on the world around him.

Our footprint does matter. The fork in the road that we choose is critical. The choices that we make can be game changing. Our attitude and the way we carry ourselves is a reflection of our inner character. So often we fail to realize the impact that we have on the lives of others. This point is hammered home in another one of my all time favorites, *It's a Wonderful Life*, with Jimmy Stewart. Jimmy plays George Bailey, a dreamer. George was always the person that put himself before others. He was the unsung hero in life. He never realized his dream, or so he thought. One day George hit one of life's potholes. He was in danger of losing whatever fortune he had earned. Struggling with doubt and a lack of self-confidence, he wished he had never been born. Ask and you shall receive. Clarence, his guardian angel, granted his wish and took him down the road to discover what life would have looked like if he were never born. George quickly realized that his *modest accomplishments in life were monumental in the eyes and the lives of others.* He realized that he was the pebble thrown into the pond. From his vantage point, he saw minimal impact. However, the ripples were far reaching. His dream and fortune were right in front of him, and nobody could ever take that away from him. He realized that he had his sprinkles all along. He realized that his sprinkles were far reaching.

Finding your sprinkles can happen early. It can happen late in life. It happens when all your stars align. It happens when your kitchen is truly in order. It happens when you assemble all the right ingredients. It's the glow in the fire. It's the last color that completes the rainbow. It's the difference between good and great. It happens when your pantry is fully equipped. One thing's for sure. Your mind and spirit must be open to the idea of realizing your preordained spot in life. You have to be willing to assemble all the ingredients, all the steps, and put the pieces together. You must have faith that your senses will safely guide you in the proper direction. Sprinkles are the missing piece to the puzzle. They complete the picture. They add sense and order to the world. They cast away doubt and bring never ending sunshine to your life. Everything is better with sprinkles on top.

In the end, the choice is yours. It's your choice to accept that you have the ultimate power to make a positive change in your life. Powerful choices lead to cascading positive returns. Choice leads to acceptance. Acceptance leads to a state of contentment. Contentment is the birthplace of enlightenment. Once you are truly enlightened and in tune with the world around you, you can find your sprinkles.

This is my wish for you. I wish for a life of abundance for all. Let's join in a sprinkle revolution. Let's rekindle our fire and spirit. Let's strive to be all we can be, every day. Let's waste little time on frivolous pursuits. Let's focus and hone in on what's truly important, you and those around you. May you find your true sprinkles in life and bless the rest of the world by sharing.

Mott-Ohs

Everything in life emanates from center; it's best to take care of yours.

I truly believe that behind every shining star in life, there is a great coach.

It's ever so important to pay attention in life.

You may be able to buy the spark, but you will never be able to buy the fire.

Sprinkles are always within your reach.

Modest accomplishments in life are monumental in the eyes of others.

Find Your Sprinkles is also available in the following formats:

E-book

Six CD audio presentation

MP-3 download

Visit www.findyoursprinkles.com to order other versions.

Thank you once again for your purchase. I hope you have enjoyed reading *Find Your Sprinkles*.

A portion of all sales will be donated to the fight against cancer.

Here's to finding your sprinkles!

In loving memory of Phyllis Mott, Gordon Hinkley, and Sandra Contrino – some of the best parents and coaches on the planet. You will be forever missed.

All the best,

Chris Mott

8905161R10122

Made in the USA
San Bernardino, CA
27 February 2014